COOKING THE ITALIAN WAY

COOKING

THE ITALIAN WAY

Dorothy Daly

PAUL HAMLYN · LONDON

First published 1958
Revised edition 1960
Paperback edition 1962

© *Paul Hamlyn Ltd 1958*

WESTBOOK HOUSE · FULHAM BROADWAY · LONDON

Printed in Czechoslovakia

T 887

Contents

Introduction

Before trying Italian cooking, it's as well to give some thoughts to the good foods native to that sunny country.

And before getting down to the food itself, give some consideration to what, in Italy, is its essential accompaniment — good wine. From north to south whether one travels by road or by rail, one doesn't go far without seeing stretches of vineyards, and from the delightful Soave, produced in the vicinity of Verona, to the slightly spicy Orvieto of the Umbrian Hills, down to the delicate Lachrima Christi with which the visitor to Naples, Pompeii and Amalfi is regaled, there's no excuse in Italy for stinting the wine with which to cook or with which to eat the finished dish. Not all Italian wines travel well enough to allow them to be brought across to our own country, but a little patient exploration will result in a fairly lengthy list of Italian wines that can be purchased here at a price sufficiently reasonable as to make it not an extravagance to use them when suggested in the recipe for a truly Italian dish, or to form the highly agreeable habit of taking a glass or two of *Vino* with one's Pasta or Ossobuco. Make the acquaintance of your Italian wine merchant; talk to him about his various wines, ask him to suggest good wines for certain dishes; get him talking about the different wines to be met with in different parts of his beloved country — if he's a true Italian, his advice will be well worth taking, and the next time you visit his country you will order your wine by name, instead of mumbling something about 'half a bottle of that red stuff'. And in spite of the long list of 'named' varieties, your Italian wine merchant will probably point to the wisdom of buying a carafe of the local wine, for many of these local wines, though they do not travel well, are excellent when drunk in their own particular place of origin.

Not only is Italy a country of wines, it is also a country of cheeses, cheeses of a staggering variety. There is no need at all in Italy to ruin an otherwise perfect dish by the addition of two tablespoons of grated 'mousetrap', nor is there any need nowadays to commit such a solecism when a fairly

good range of Italian cheeses may be found in the best provision shops of most large towns. Where cheese for cooking
is concerned, we may have to substitute Bel Paese, which
travels well, for Mozzarella, which doesn't, and cream cheese
for the Italian Ricotta which again doesn't care much for
transportation, but where table cheeses are concerned, there's
a wide variety from which to choose.

And what of the olive groves, where the silvery-grey leaves
of the slender gnarled trees give an other-world appearance
to the landscape? Small wonder that so many truly Italian
dishes are built upon a foundation of either the fruit, green
or ripened to blackness, or the oil extracted from the fruit
of these trees — and remember, the use of oil in cooking
does not mean that the resulting dish will be oily — only the
badly cooked dish merits that adjective.

Wines, cheeses, olive oil, lemons, lemon juice and tomatoes
(raw, cooked or rendered down into the purée or conserve we
can now purchase in 'tooth-paste' tubes that allow one to use
a little without wasting the balance), green, red, yellow and
variegated peppers, purple aubergines, artichokes, and
zucchini are but a few of the colourful basic foods of the
peninsula, but they are enough to go on with.

And why, so far, no word of *Pasta*, that ever-present, ubi-
quitous Italian dish? For the reason that *Pasta*, whatever it
may be to-day, is said not originally to have been a native of
the country, but is alleged to be one of the many wonders
brought home by the thirteenth century explorer, Marco
Polo, from his travels in China. Nevertheless, although *Pasta*,
in its many shapes and forms, may not have started off as
a true native of Italy, to-day it seems as much a part of the
country as an operatic tenor, and anyone wanting to present
a truly Italian meal must perforce learn a few of the ways
of preparing and cooking *Pasta*.

So much for the food and drink harvested from the land.
What about the fruit of the seas that wash the shores of the
long, indented coastline, all the strange and lovely fish and
shellfish abounding in the waters? What of the colourful fish
to be seen in the fish market in Venice, to mention but one
of the famous markets? In most coastal towns of Italy fish is
good and recipes for cooking it abound. Your taste won't,

of course, take kindly to all of them, and the mention of octopus may bring forth a horrified shudder, but few people look askance at a dish of scampi or red mullet, and these are but two of a great number of delicacies piscatorial.

In the following pages an attempt has been made to offer a selection of typical Italian dishes that can be cooked and enjoyed in our own country. It is a compilation rather than an invention, for to 'invent' four hundred 'original' Italian recipes would be not merely an impossible task but an insult to the established repertoire of Italian cooks.

Some Useful Facts and Figures

Comparison of English and American Weights and Measures

English weights and measures have been used throughout this book. 3 teaspoonfuls equal 1 tablespoon. The average English teacup is ¼ pint or 1 gill. The average English breakfast cup is ½ pint or 2 gills. When cups are mentioned in recipes they refer to a B.S.I. measuring cup which holds ½ pint or fluid ounces. The B.S.I. standard tablespoon measures 1 fluid ounce.

In case it is wished to translate any of the weights and measures into their American, Canadian or French counterparts, the following tables give a comparison.

Solid Measure

ENGLISH	AMERICAN
1 lb. Butter or other fat	2 cups
1 lb. Flour	4 cups
1 lb. Granulated or Castor Sugar	2 cups
1 lb. Brown (moist) Sugar	2⅓ cups
1 lb. Icing or Confectioner's Sugar	3 cups
1 lb. Syrup or Treacle	1 cup
1 lb. Dried Fruit	2 cups
1 lb. Chopped Meat (finely packed)	2 cups
1 lb. Lentils or Split Peas	2 cups
1 lb. Coffee (unground)	2⅔ cups
1 lb. Breadcrumbs	4 cups
½ oz. Flour	1 level tablespoon
1 oz. Flour	1 heaped tablespoon
1 oz. Syrup or Treacle	1 tablespoon
1 oz. Sugar	1 level tablespoon
1 oz. Jam or Jelly	1 level tablespoon
½ oz. Butter	1 tablespoon smoothed off

Liquid measure

The most important difference to be noted is that the American and Canadian pint is 16 fluid ounces, as opposed to the British Imperial pint, which is 20 fluid ounces. The American ½-pint measuring cup is therefore actually equivalent to two-fifths of a British pint.

French Weights and Measures

It is difficult to convert to French measures with absolute accuracy, but 1 oz. is equal to approximately 30 grammes, 2 lb. 3 oz. to 1 kilogramme. For liquid measure, approximately 1¾ English pints may be regarded as equal to 1 litre; 1 demilitre is half a litre, and 1 décilitre is one-tenth of a litre.

Oven Temperatures

	Electricity °F.	Gas regulo	°C
COOL	225 to 250	0 to ½	107—121
VERY SLOW	250 to 275	½ to 1	121—135
SLOW	275 to 300	1 to 2	135—149
VERY MODERATE	300 to 350	2 to 3	149—177
MODERATE	375	4	190
MODERATELY HOT	400	5	204
HOT	425 to 450	6 to 7	218—233
VERY HOT	475 to 500	8 to 9	246—260

Note. This table is an approximate guide only. Different makes of cooker vary and if you are in any doubt about the setting it is as well to refer to the manufacturer's temperature chart.

Flavourings, Trimmings, Herbs and Spices Used in Italian Cookery

In the Italian kitchen herbs and spices play an important part, and a chapter is not too much to devote to their nature and uses. Taking them alphabetically the following is a fairly comprehensive list: —

BAY: Although it is possible to purchase dried bay leaves at most herbal stores and at some chemists' shops, their flavour is nothing to be compared with that of a freshly plucked leaf, and since the shrubs grow well in tubs and, except for adequate watering, need little care or attention, why not grow your own? They make an attractive addition to any garden, and even in a small yard or balcony there is room for a small tub of bay. If your house stands far enough back from the street, a tub of bay each side of the front door is attractive, and at the same time provides a useful means of adding to your flavouring ingredients.

A leaf of bay in a risotto — removed before serving — or in a casserole of meat or fish, or even as an added flavour to the béchamel base for cream soups is an excellent idea.

BASIL: Basil is a little known herb yet its cultivation is not difficult. It grows in profusion in Southern Italy where it is used as a fragrant and welcome addition to most dishes where tomatoes are used, chopped finely — or preferably torn into fine shreds with the fingers — and added to a green salad, and it also takes its place as a delicate and unusual flavouring in some egg dishes and soups.

In attempting to grow this delicious herb in your own garden, remember the heat and sunshine of Italy where it thrives, and choose a sunny corner of your plot or a sunny window-box for your experiment. If, in spite of all your care, it refuses to flourish, it is possible to buy the dried herb from most herb stores, but as with all dried leaf herbs, it is at best a poor substitute for the leaves of the growing plant.

BORAGE: This is a herb we associate mainly with wine cups, but in parts of Italy it is used as a flavouring ingredient, sometimes it finds its way into the filling for ravioli, sometimes, finely chopped, a sprinkling is added to a green salad, and its flavour combines excellently with that of cucumbers. It is a plant that grows wild on the English Sussex Downs, but if these are inaccessible to you, it is possible to purchase it at some, though not all, herb shops. It is advisable to use it soon after it is picked, as it has a tendency to wither quickly.

BREADCRUMBS: It is an excellent idea to get into the habit of slicing thinly any left-over stale bread, drying it out in the bottom of the oven when baking, and when it is crisp grinding it into fine crumbs so that one is never without a jar of these ready at hand to be used as a coating for fried foods, or sprinkled, together with grated cheese, on top of a baked fish dish, or as a thickening ingredient for various stuffings.

CELERY: The Italian climate does not appear to produce such a deliciously crisp 'eating' celery as we are accustomed to, for which reason it rarely makes an appearance in its raw state in that country, but stalks and even the inner, tender leaves are used as flavouring ingredients in soups and stews.

And here is a hint, not native to Italy, but worth remembering when celery is out of season. Instead of discarding the tougher, outer stalks, scrub these clean, wipe them dry, and cut into inch lengths. Spread on a tin and dry slowly — on the floor of a slow oven, or on top of your kitchen boiler. When quite dry, store in a screw-top jar, and use as a flavouring for soups when fresh celery is no longer available. The dried stalks can also be used as a flavouring ingredient in stews, but in this case it is best to tie them in a piece of muslin, so that they can be removed before the dish is served, as they are unattractive to the eye once they have been dried.

CHEESE: The variety of Italian 'table' cheeses is extensive, but there are three 'cooking cheeses' the names of which appear time after time in Italian recipes.

Of these three, the best known is Parmesan, the apparently high cost of which has alarmed more than one inexperienced housewife. Actually, in practice, this cheese works out not at all extravagantly, for its texture is so close, its flavour so concentrated that a very little of it when grated will produce sufficient to go a long way. Do not be tempted to go about the use of Parmesan the 'easy' way by purchasing it already ground. If you buy a small lump, even as little as two ounces in weight, and grate it freshly for each occasion, the flavour is richer and the cost less than if you rely on the commercially ground variety.

Another cheese frequently mentioned is Mozzarella, a cheese made from buffalo milk, which unfortunately does not stand up to export, and consequently is not to be found in this country. It is fairly safe to substitute Bel Paese wherever a recipe mentions Mozzarella, and Bel Paese is obtainable in most good provision stores nowadays.

The third cheese for which we need to think up a substitute is the sheep's milk cheese, Ricotta, met with in Southern Italy, a cheese that when fresh possesses a deliciously pungent flavour, but which, as with Mozzarella, does not stand up to export or long keeping. As its consistency is much the same as our own sour milk cottage cheese, although the suggestion might sound like rank heresy to an Italian cook, cottage cheese is a fairly safe substitute wherever Ricotta is prescribed.

FENNEL: The root of this vegetable, thinly sliced, forms a frequent ingredient in salads, particularly in and around Venice, where I have often mistaken it at first bite for the heart of celery by reason of its somewhat similar appearance and texture. A second bite, however, disproves this, for there is a slight flavour of aniseed to fennel, which is absent from celery.

Sliced thinly and sprinkled with salt and marinated in olive oil, fennel is sometimes served as a tit-bit at the end of a meal.

We and the French use the leaves of fennel as a flavouring ingredient far more than does the Italian cook; take for example the delicious fennel sauce served as an adjunct to boiled fish — particularly salmon, and the French use of it as a flavouring for soups and stews. But, except for the districts around Perugia and Gubbio and other cities of the province of Umbria, the stalk and leaves rarely find their way into Italian recipes. The Umbrians are fond of using fennel to flavour the stuffing used in roast sucking pig.

FISH, TINNED OR SALTED: Anchovies, sardines, and tunny are frequent ingredients in Italian cookery, and it is a good idea to keep a stock of all three in your store cupboard.

GARLIC: Yes, I know, we've all encountered that garlic-laden breath that has given rise to the legend that all Italian food is heavily laced with this odorous bulb, but legend notwithstanding, the best type of Italian cooking prescribes no more than a discreet use of this pungent member of the onion family.

It is now possible to purchase a garlic crusher, made on the principle of a potato ricer, which enables a few drops of garlic juice to be added to a dish rather than a too-coarsely chopped clove. These presses are not cheap, but in labour-saving and flavour-refinement are a worthwhile investment.

Certainly in and around Naples the use of garlic in dishes made from tomatoes and in soups is somewhat lavish, and the Neapolitans have a fondness for a dish of spaghetti flavoured with nothing more than good, fresh olive oil and garlic (here is an instance where your garlic press will give good service), but in the main, the use of garlic in Italian cooking is tempered with more restraint than rumour would have one believe.

JUNIPER BERRIES: Used discreetly, these form an interesting addition to the stuffing for pork or game.

MARJORAM with which may be classed the elusive herb OREGANO, mentioned in so many Italian recipes, which is the wild marjoram similar to that which grows on the English Downs:

Either the sweet marjoram, which is easily procurable from a herb shop, and which many of us grow in our gardens, or the wild is a welcome addition to many Italian dishes, to soups, and fish dishes, while a pinch in an *Omelette aux fines herbes* does not come amiss. As with all herbs, the fresh product, when obtainable, is infinitely preferable to the dried.

MINT: In English cookery it usually means the mint sauce eaten with roast lamb, or a sprig or two to be boiled with new potatoes or with spring peas, and that, except for the Lancashire mint and currant pasty, is the extent to which the English use it. The Italian cook makes a far wider use of the herb, particularly in and around Rome where it makes a fairly frequent appearance as a flavouring to soups, fish dishes, stews and salads.

MUSHROOMS: Dried mushrooms — uninteresting though they may look hanging in strings in an Italian provision shop — are excellent used in small quantities in many soups and sauces. Before use they should first be soaked in warm water to soften them, and added to the dish 15 to 20 minutes before serving time. Overcooked they tend to lose their flavour and their texture is flabby.

MYRTLE: The sweet-smelling myrtle of Southern Italy and Sicily has a stronger odour than the English variety. It is used less in Italy as a flavouring ingredient than on the island of Sardinia.

OLIVE OIL: All too frequently, alas, one meets the one-voyage-abroad traveller who complains of Italian food that it is 'much too oily' and one feels that the cooking of the country has once again been let down by the wrong kind of restaurant, for though the Italian cook uses olive oil lavishly for deep frying, for salads, as a dressing for pasta, etc., provided the oil and the cook are of first quality, the resulting dish is not oily in the objectionable sense, but rich, fragrant and delicious.

The oil, however, must be olive oil of the best quality, and the temptation to substitute an anonymous product making its appearance under the name of 'frying oil' is one to be sternly resisted. Until you know your oils, it is advisable to spend your money on a named brand, the *San Remo*, for example. Get accustomed to using a good oil, to recognising its flavour and its cooking qualities, and later you may safely experiment with less well-known brands, but even then, insist that the oil you use must be olive oil, for just as the grey green foliage of the olive tree is an essential feature of the Italian landscape, so is the oil of its fruit an essential feature of Italian cookery.

PARSLEY: It is used lavishly by Italian cooks, in soups, in salads, as an ingredient for the stuffings for meats, vegetables and the various forms of ravioli. If you are able to obtain a package of seeds of the true Italian parsley, try growing this instead of or in addition to the English variety. The leaf is flatter, thinner and less curly, so that for decorative purposes the English plant may be preferable, but the flavour of the Italian parsley is considerably stronger and more poignant and for that reason I would recommend its use whenever possible.

PINE NUTS: Do experiment with these, which are stocked by most vegetarian stores. A few chopped and added to a sour-sweet sauce, or used in place of almonds in cake-making, or instead of salted almonds to be served with drinks, will reward your courage.

ROSEMARY: It is a herb we tend to think of in conjunction with the word *Remembrance* or even, alas, as an ingredient for hair tonic; as a cooking ingredient it seems alien to our taste. However, chopped and used sparingly, since it is extremely pungent, either fresh or dried it is delicious sprinkled over sauté potatoes during cooking, or again used cautiously to flavour a roast of veal, pork or lamb. In some of the Italian food markets you will see rolled fillets of meat already prepared for roasting and lavishly trimmed with this herb, but for non-Italian tastes a little of it goes a fairly long way.

This again is a herb that can be grown in one's own garden, and once again you'll find that a pinch of the fresh is worth a peck of the dried.

SAFFRON: This is used mainly to produce a delicate yellow colour in some rice dishes, rather as in Cornwall it is used to produce a similar yellow tint in the saffron buns for which that county is noted.

The dried stamens of the Autumn Crocus give us the true saffron and when one remembers that there are but three stamens to one flower, it can be realised what an extensive cultivation of the flower is necessary to produce a very little supply of saffron. If you are working with the dried stamens, take three or four of these, bruise them to a powder, and allow them to steep in a little hot water or soup for five or six minutes before adding the strained liquid to the dish you are colouring. A quicker method is to purchase, literally, a thimbleful of powdered saffron and experiment by adding it a pinch at a time until you have obtained the desired colour.

The flavour of saffron is so delicate that it is apt to be obscured by the stronger predominating flavours of the dish so that, preferable though it always is to use the true product, in this case, the substitution of a manufactured imitation does not materially affect the taste of the finished dish.

SAGE: Although this herb is used less in Italian cooking than in our own, it is occasionally mentioned in a recipe. Because of its heavy under-taste, it is to many lovers of Italian cooking less attractive than basil or wild marjoram.

SALT: Here is a case where I would urge you to forsake the nicely packed, beautifully ground commercial salt and to try the experiment of using the sea salt that can be purchased from the provisions department of most big stores. There are wooden salt mills that can be used at table for adding this salt to cooked food, and once tried, these are usually preferred to the trickle — or in our damp climate, the frequent lack-of-trickle — of commercial salt from a salt shaker or salt spoon.

SPICES — a few of the most common.

Cinnamon: Instead of confining its use to cakes and apple dishes, try the occasional pinch in a meat or vegetable dish.
Cloves: Some Italian cookery books prescribe a pinch, a very modest pinch, of this aromatic herb in stewed meat or meat sauces, and it is a tip worth trying.
Coriander seeds: Keep a small jar of these in your spice cupboard and try one or two crushed as a flavouring for roast meat.
Fennel seeds: These are used for flavouring far more than are the leaves and stalks of the raw plant and there is a specially delicious kind of salami, native to the city of Florence which takes its name *finocchiona* from the fact that fennel seeds are predominant in its flavouring ingredients.

18

In some parts of Italy and Sicily these seeds are used also as a flavouring for dried figs.

Nutmeg: By all means continue to use this spice as a flavouring in milk dishes, but do experiment now and again with the wider use of it — a pinch in a meat stew, or in potato soup, or in any dish using spinach makes a welcome addition.

Pepper: If you have not yet forsaken the commercially packaged ready ground pepper for the pleasure of grinding peppercorns in your own pepper mill, I cannot too strongly urge you to do so without delay. The improvement in flavour is almost unbelievable.

TARRAGON: It is not always easy to procure this herb, but a leaf or two in a salad is a reward for the effort of running it to earth, while the delicate flavour of tarragon vinegar once acquired is preferred by many to the cruder taste of plain malt vinegar in salads.

THYME: Although in Southern Italy and in Sicily one often comes across this herb growing wild, and after a sprinkling of rain finds the air drenched with its fragrance, it is not used very much in cooking. It can, however, be used in restricted doses wherever oregano has been suggested if this is unobtainable or difficult to find.

TOMATOES: Where tomatoes are concerned, as a general rule the tinned varieties imported from Italy are preferable to our own fresh, local grown tomatoes.

In any dish calling for raw tomatoes, ours are excellent, but for cooked dishes, sauces, stews, soups, etc., I would every time recommend the tinned, peeled tomatoes. The tomatoes grown in Italy are larger and softer than those we grow here, their flavour is richer, and their colour deeper. One of the most popular and easily-obtainable brands is the *Cirio*, but there are several others to be purchased in provision stores if this particular brand is not available.

Concentrated tomato paste is another ingredient appearing again in Italian recipes, and after years of experimenting, a method of packaging this has been evolved that is practical and non-wasteful, for it can now be purchased in metal tubes, rather after the fashion of toothpaste, so that when a little has been used, the tube can be sealed and the remainder kept without danger of spoiling. Previously this paste used to appear in microscopic tins which had a fiendish knack of defeating even the best tin-opener, particularly if the cook happened to be working against time. Another former method of packaging was in small blocks wrapped in oiled paper, which, because of the high degree of concentration of the paste, necessitated a fair amount of pounding to reduce them to a usable consistency. It is still possible to purchase the paste in these forms, but the tubed variety is infinitely easier to handle.

Do not fall into the trap of using this paste too lavishly, for while a little is excellent, too much can result in an overflavouring that tends to kill the other flavours of any dish.

Antipasti

Antipasti is the name given to the large variety of tit-bits, or hors-d'oeuvre which, in a truly Italian household, are served as a prelude to pasta or soup. They may consist of a few wafer-thin slices of salami with a garnish of a couple of anchovies and a few black olives, or they may be considerably more elaborate, but whatever their nature they must be interesting to look at and appetising to taste. Some of the following suggestions may fill you with apprehension; for instance, boiled rice combined with grated carrots, or the slice of ham to be eaten with an ice cold slice of honeydew melon, or with a couple of ripe figs, but taste and try, and you'll probably come back for more.

ANTIPASTI MADE WITH RICE

Really delicious antipasti can be concocted starting with a basis of plain boiled rice.

Allow 1 tablespoon of rice per person, and boil in salted water as directed on page 95. Drain and before it is quite cold season with a tablespoon of olive oil to each tablespoon of uncooked rice, freshly ground black pepper, more salt if needed, and a teaspoon of lemon juice or wine vinegar, plus a suspicion of finely chopped or crushed garlic, or a few shavings — very thin — of onion. Allow to become quite cold, then mix with any of the following, or a combination of two or three of them:

Grated raw carrot — using half as much carrot as rice.

Finely shredded raw green peppers — quantity as for carrot.

Tunny fish broken small with a fork, equal quantities of fish and rice, and even better with the addition of one anchovy per tablespoon of tunny fish.

Finely chopped green olives, half as much as rice.

Whole black olives, four or five per tablespoon of rice.

Minced cold chicken, equal quantities with rice.

Mushrooms, raw or cooked in equal quantities.

Fresh peeled shrimps or prawns, or if available, scampi, and to enhance these, add also a generous amount of freshly chopped parsley and a few cooked green peas or French beans.

Chopped celery hearts, finely chopped fennel, finely sliced preserved artichoke hearts in equal quantities with the rice, are three other alternatives, and with these try the addition of a few blanched and chopped almonds or pine nuts.

Using the foregoing suggestions as a basis, you should be able to utilise left-over boiled rice to good advantage to produce an interesting hors-d'oeuvre.

HARICOT OR BUTTER BEANS WITH FISH

It is now possible to buy cooked butter beans in tins, or alternatively you may use the small white haricot beans, remembering, however, that these need soaking overnight, and then boiling for quite three hours the following day before they are tender. Whichever you decide to use, drain and marinate with a little under a tablespoon of olive oil to a tablespoon of beans, seasoning with salt, pepper and a little grated onion, and a little lemon juice or vinegar. Serve with equal quantities of flaked tunny fish, very cold.

FENNEL ANTIPASTO

head of fennel
3 tablespoons olive oil
1 tablespoon lemon
  juice

freshly ground
  black pepper
salt

Wash a head of fennel, and soak in very cold water for 2 or 3 hours to allow it to become crisp. Slice thinly, and pile in a dish. With it hand the above dressing, into which the fennel is dipped before eating.

STUFFED FENNEL OR CELERY

Wash the tender stalks of either of these, soak in cold water to allow them to become crisp, and before serving spread with cottage cheese, pounded anchovies, or a combination of the two.

OTHER WAYS WITH FENNEL

Try combining thinly sliced fennel with thinly sliced crisp red radishes, or with thinly sliced unpeeled cucumber, in each case serving with a dressing of oil, lemon juice, pepper and salt, and a sprinkling of parsley, or mint finely chopped.

FORTUNATA RUOCCO'S COLD PEPPER ANTIPASTO

To each person allow:

1 pepper (assorted colours make the finished dish
   more attractive)
1 small teaspoon best olive oil
½ lemon
a scraping of garlic

Prepare your peppers by baking them whole in a fireproof dish placed in a larger dish with water halfway the height of the dish containing the peppers. Cook until the skins are wrinkled — about 45 minutes in a hot oven.

Cool slightly, peel off the thin outer skin, cut in two and remove all the seeds. Slice thinly, and arrange on a serving dish, alternating the colours if you have been able to procure peppers of varied colours. Sprinkle with a scraping of garlic, and marinate with olive oil. Cool thoroughly before serving, and allow a ½ lemon per person when the finished dish is served.

Hot Antipasti

In addition to the galaxy of ideas for cold antipasti, or hors-d'oeuvre, our Italian friends are fond of serving delicious little hot tit-bits that take the same place in the repast as the cold antipasti, and are a trifle less chilling on a cool day. Here are suggestions for some of these, which can also make their bow as rich little savouries to be served with drinks.

CHICKEN TARTLETS

Into a little rich béchamel sauce (see page 214) mix 2 table-spoons grated Parmesan, and 4 oz. or more of cold cooked chicken, cut into small pieces, a few chopped mushrooms, and a slice of lean ham cut small. Mix well together, and use as a filling for tartlets.

CHICKEN LIVER TARTLETS

This time, impregnate your béchamel with chopped chicken livers that have been cooked in a little Marsala, and to this add chopped mushrooms and seasonings. Mix well and use to fill small pastry tartlets.

STUFFED MUSHROOMS

Choose the small 'button' mushrooms, and allow three or four per person.

Peel, and remove the stalks, setting the stalks aside to be added to soup stock or tomato sauce — *don't* waste them, whatever you do, they are far too good a flavouring. Sauté the mushrooms in hot butter; meanwhile heat the contents of a small tin of anchovies, and when the mushrooms are cooked, place a curled anchovy inside each mushroom (the dark side is the side to receive the anchovy). Serve on toothpicks while still very hot.

ANCHOVY TOAST
TO SERVE 4

Mash to a paste the contents of a small tin of anchovies, mixing with a little melted butter. Prepare some slices of bread about 4 inches by 2 inches, and toast on one side only. On the other side spread the anchovy paste fairly thickly, sprinkle with grated Parmesan, and if liked a few chopped green olives. Brown under a hot grill and serve while piping hot.

HOT ANTIPASTO MADE WITH
GREEN PEPPERS

For each person allow:

1 green pepper	a suspicion of garlic
1 peeled tomato	a few drops of oil
6 capers	from the anchovies
2 or more anchovies	

Remove the seeds from the peppers after having sliced off the top; stuff the cavity with tomato, add garlic, anchovies, capers, and a few drops of the oil from the anchovies. Replace the top of each pepper.

Arrange in a fire proof deep dish and bake in a medium-hot oven for 45 minutes, basting at intervals with the balance of the oil from the tin of anchovies and a little hot water.

Serve before or in place of soup, very hot.

These are even more attractive if baked in individual fireproof dishes.

PANDORATO ALLA ROMANA
Fried bread in the Roman fashion

For this recipe, allow 1 or 2½-inch slices of bread per person, and remove the crusts so that your slices are about 3 inches square.

You will need also a little warmed milk, 1 or 2 beaten eggs, depending on the number of slices, salt for seasoning, and oil for frying.

An hour before starting to cook the slices, spread them in a single layer in a large flat dish and sprinkle them with warm milk, and then with sufficient beaten egg to soak the bread without making it soggy. Leave for an hour, then lift each slice gently with a spatula and fry in hot oil, first on one side then on the other until golden brown.

FRIED BREAD WITH ANCHOVIES

Allow 1 or 1½ slices of bread per person; cut the slices about ½ inch thick, remove the crusts and cut in two, lengthways. To each strip of bread allow a little Bel Paese and half an anchovy and for the whole dish allow 1 or 2 eggs depending on the quantity of bread to be prepared. You will need also pepper and salt for seasoning, flour and oil for frying.

On half the number of strips of bread spread a layer of Bel Paese, and on that lay a ½ anchovy cut into small pieces. Season with pepper, and cover with the second slice.

Heat the oil in a pan, and meanwhile dip the sandwiches first of all in water or a little milk, then in flour and finally in beaten egg, and fry quickly, first on one side and then on the other until golden brown. Serve very hot.

CROSTINI ALLA NAPOLITANA

For each person allow 2 slices of bread, ½ inch thick, with crusts removed and cut in two lengthways, and for each slice of bread allow one anchovy, a little Bel Paese and a ½ tomato skinned and with the seeds removed. Allow a little oregano and pepper for seasoning.

Fry the pieces of bread in hot oil on one side only, then arrange in a single layer in a greased flat fireproof dish, fried side uppermost. On each slice spread a layer of Bel Paese, a ½ anchovy cut small and a thin slice or two of tomato, and finally sprinkle with oregano and black pepper and a few drops of olive oil.

Cook in a hot oven for 10 minutes to allow the cheese to melt. Serve very hot.

PANDORATO ALLA CREMA DI FORMAGGIO

Fried bread with cheese cream

TO SERVE 4

6 slices of bread ½ inch thick, with crusts removed
and cut in two lengthways

4 oz. Gruyère cheese
½ pint milk, or a little
   more
olive oil for frying

a walnut of butter
2 eggs, separated
flour

Whip the whites of eggs. Having prepared the strips of
bread, dip them first in water or a little milk, then in flour,
then in the whipped egg whites; fry them in hot olive oil and
when golden brown, lay in a flat fireproof dish and cover
with the following cheese cream:

Cut the cheese in small pieces and place in a basin, and cover
with the milk and leave for quite an hour, by the end of which
time the cheese will have softened. Place it in a double boiler,
add the beaten egg yolks and stir with a wooden spoon until
the whole is mixed well and has become a thick cream.
Remove from the fire and stir in a knob of butter the size
of a walnut.

Spread this cream over the slices of fried bread and serve
hot, garnished with sprigs of parsley.

FRIED GREEN OLIVES

3—4 large Spanish
  olives per person
a thick slice of bread
  with the crust
  removed

1 anchovy to each
  4 olives
flour
pepper and salt
batter and oil for frying

Peel the olives in a spiral so that you can remove the stone without breaking the flesh; soak the bread in a little water, and when it has become saturated, squeeze it dry in the hand; one slice should be sufficient for half a dozen anchovies. Remove the bones from the anchovies and pound them in a mortar, together with the bread, a few drops of olive oil and season them with freshly ground black pepper. When they are reduced to a paste, stuff the cavities of the olives with the mixture, then dip in flour, and after that into a thin batter, and fry in hot olive oil. Drain well before serving.

Soups

Soup forms an integral part of the daily diet of Italy, and the variety of Italian soups is considerable.

Starting with a basis of chicken or meat stock, we have several plain, clear broths, of the consommé type, we have the ever-popular *minestrone* type, where the stock is laced with an assortment of vegetables, eked out with dried peas or beans, and occasionally meat, and there are the various forms of *pasta in brodo*.

The Italian verb *minestrare* — to serve up soup — derives from a similar Latin verb *minestrare* which has the fuller meaning of *putting food on the table*, and it must be admitted that when a bowl of really good minestrone is placed before one, it has the appearance of a meal in itself, and could well serve as such, since there seems to be no end to the many ingredients that can find their way into this tasty and typically Italian dish, and all to its betterment.

Pasta in brodo is the term applied to a generous portion of any of the large variety of pastas, cooked and served in hot broth, and taking the same place in the menu as the *pasta asciutta*, or dry pasta, cooked and served with various sauces, with which we have dealt in the section headed *Pasta* (see page 53).

The variety of fish soups in the Italian cook's repertoire is far greater than in our own, and although cream soups and purées were originally more used in France than in Italy, with the passage of years a fairly large number of recipes for these have found their way into Italian cookery books, adapted and amended so that they now pass as very nearly native to the country of their adoption.

Where the consommés, the minestre, and the *pasta in brodo* are concerned, although the family stockpot is not absolutely essential, it is strongly to be recommended if time and space permit. There are, it is true, some truly excellent chicken and beef bouillon cubes now obtainable in good provision stores, but the best of these is but a substitute for the broth resulting from the operation of a well-run stock-pot. For that reason I am starting the recipes of this section with two suggestions for soup stock.

STOCK FOR CLEAR SOUP

2 lb. lean beef - shin of
  beef is excellent
2 quarts cold water
1 small onion
a few stalks of celery

4 cloves stuck into the
  onion
6 whole peppercorns
1 bay leaf
salt, pepper and sprig
  parsley

Cut meat small, place in a stew pan and cover with cold water and bring slowly to the boil. Skim off any scum that rises to the top with a perforated spoon. Cover stewpan closely and let it simmer slowly for 6 hours or rather more. Strain, cool and remove fat. Replace in pan, adding onion stuck with cloves and celery cut small, parsley, peppercorns and bay leaf. Simmer for a further 20 minutes after bringing to the boil. Add salt and pepper to taste. Strain through a cloth.

This is an excellent basis for any clear soup, to which may be added *pasta* for a dish of *pasta in brodo*, rice, or pearl barley.

HOUSEHOLD STOCK POT

· 3 quarts cold water
3 lb. meat: trimmings
  from steak, bones,
  etc. and the addition
  of a ham bone or
  bacon knuckle bone
  is excellent

1 small onion stuck with
  4 cloves
6 peppercorns
parsley
1 stalk celery, chopped
  small
salt and pepper

This is a stock that may be used as a foundation for many kinds of soups or sauces, for casserole dishes, etc.

Place meat in a stewpan and cover with cold water and bring slowly to the boil, skimming well. Cover and simmer for 5 hours, or longer, add balance of ingredients and simmer 1 hour more. Add salt and pepper to taste, being chary of adding too much salt if you have among your meat a ham or bacon bone. Strain and set aside to cool. Remove the fat before using.

Brought to the boil once daily, this stock will last for several days without spoiling.

CHICKEN BROTH

TO SERVE 6

1 boiling fowl	1 pinch thyme
2 carrots	a dash of nutmeg,
1 onion	salt and pepper to
3 stalks celery	taste
1 tablespoon chopped	4 quarts water
parsley	

Place all ingredients in saucepan, bring to boil and skim; lower heat and simmer for 2 hours or until fowl is tender. Remove fowl, strain soup through a fine sieve, allow to cool and remove fat. Reheat. This is a good basic soup for any of the varieties of pasta in brodo.

Try it with Cappelletti (filled pasta — see pages 58 and 74) filled with the following mixture:

the breast of the boiled	1 egg plus 1 egg yolk
chicken chopped fine	3 tablespoons grated
8 oz. cottage cheese	Parmesan
2 tablespoons butter	salt and pepper

Mix well together and use as filling for Cappelletti. Drop into boiling chicken broth 5 or 6 minutes before serving.

CREAM SOUPS

Where cream soups are concerned the starting point is a good, rich béchamel sauce, thinner than used when intended purely as a sauce, but made with care and using the best ingredients, butter, flour, milk and seasonings. The following is a good, reliable recipe for a béchamel to be used as a basis for cream soup to serve four people:

1½ to 2 oz. butter	1½ pints hot milk
2 tablespoons flour	pepper and salt

Melt the butter in a small saucepan or in the top of your double boiler, but do not allow it to brown. Add the flour and blend well together, stirring constantly to prevent its going lumpy. Add the hot milk slowly, continuing to stir. When thickened, allow to cook very slowly for a further 15 minutes, otherwise the taste of the flour will predominate. Add a little extra milk if it looks like becoming too thick, and if you are unfortunate enough to have it go lumpy, do not hesitate to pass it through a strainer, though if the flour and butter are well blended and the mixture is stirred constantly lumps should be conspicuous by their absence.

Once your béchamel is properly blended and while it is 'maturing' in the top of your double boiler, you have time to prepare the vegetables for the particular cream soup you have in mind.

A time and washing-up saver is to make the béchamel from start to finish in the top of your double boiler, rather than using a separate saucepan for the preliminary cooking and then transferring it to the top of the double boiler once the blending is completed.

One small and permissible economy that is often an improvement in flavour is to eke out the quantity of milk by substituting for $\frac{1}{3}$ or $\frac{1}{4}$ of it the hot water from a saucepan of cooking vegetables. Potato water is excellent; so is the water in which Brussels sprouts or celery are being cooked, but here it is as well to test the liquid for saltiness before adding it to the béchamel, rejecting it if it is too highly salted, unless you are prepared to eat an over-salted soup.

A REALLY GOOD MINESTRONE

TO SERVE 6

1 lb. salt pork cut small	1 small cabbage
2 quarts water, or better, beef stock	2 carrots, diced
2 tablespoons finely chopped parsley	8 oz. haricot beans, soaked overnight
1 clove crushed garlic if liked	4 oz. shelled peas
1 tablespoon butter	a few French beans
	4 tablespoons rice
	grated Parmesan
	pepper and salt

Place cut up pork in water or stock and bring to the boil before adding parsley, garlic and chopped vegetables, peas and beans. Allow to boil gently for $2\frac{1}{2}$ hours, then add rice and cook for a further quarter of an hour. Season to taste. Serve with a layer of Parmesan cheese sprinkled over the soup in the tureen.

MINESTRONE No. 2

TO SERVE 4

4 oz. salt pork cut in small pieces
1 large or 2 small onions
2 quarts water
1 large carrot
1 head celery
$\frac{1}{2}$ small spring cabbage
$\frac{1}{2}$ lettuce
8 oz. tomatoes
4 oz. French beans, cut in pieces

8 oz. shelled green peas
1 small tin sweet corn
salt and pepper to taste
4 oz. small macaroni - elbow macaroni, pastina (rice-shaped macaroni) or alphabet macaroni, small stars, or any of the small types

Fry the pork in a little lard until it is slightly brown; add onion cut small and cook till golden brown; add water and bring to the boil; add carrot and celery cut into small pieces; add shredded cabbage and lettuce, beans, peas, peeled and sliced tomatoes, corn and salt and pepper to taste. Cover and allow to cook gently for about $1\frac{1}{2}$ hours. 20 minutes before serving add the macaroni. Serve hot with hand-grated Parmesan to be added at will.

MINESTRONE No. 3
TO SERVE 4

1½ quarts water
1 lb. French beans
   or shelled peas
4 potatoes — medium
   size
8 oz. tomatoes, peeled
   and cut into small
   pieces
salt and pepper to taste

2 cloves garlic crushed
2 tablespoons chopped
   fresh basil, or if this
   is unobtainable
   2 tablespoons
   chopped parsley
1 teaspoon tomato paste
grated Parmesan
4 oz. vermicelli

Heat water to boiling point and add beans cut in pieces, or peas, together with the potatoes cut small and the tomatoes and seasoning. Cook together until vegetables are tender — about 25 minutes — then add the vermicelli and cook for a further 15 minutes or until the pasta is *al dente*. Mix together the crushed garlic, basil or parsley and tomato paste with a spoonful or two of the soup to make a smooth paste, and mix with the balance of the soup, stirring well to ensure that it is well blended.

Serve with plenty of grated Parmesan.

LENTIL SOUP WITH DRIED YELLOW LENTILS
TO SERVE 4

8 oz. dried yellow
   lentils — soaked
   overnight
1 quart stock
1 ham or gammon bone

2 medium sized onions
   chopped finely
2 tablespoons olive oil
2 celery stalks cut
   fine

Drain lentils and add to stock, add gammon bone, bring to the boil, simmer gently in a covered saucepan for 1½ hours. Remove bone and pass soup through a food mill or sieve.

Heat oil in a heavy pan and in it cook the celery and onion gently for 10 minutes.

Add to the soup and serve very hot.

MINESTRA CRÉCY

TO SERVE 4

4 medium sized carrots
(cooked in boiling
salted water and
passed through a food
mill)

1½ pints beef stock
4 tablespoons rice
salt and pepper
to taste
1 teaspoon sugar

Bring stock to the boil, add rice and boil for 20 minutes; just before serving, add puréed carrot, sugar and a knob of butter.

VEGETABLE SOUP WITH MEAT BALLS

TO SERVE 6

2 quarts stock
2 stalks of celery
2 or 3 carrots
2 medium sized
onions
1 turnip

1 tablespoon chopped
parsley
1 medium size tin
tomatoes
salt and pepper to
taste

Bring stock to the boil and add vegetables and cover. Cook gently together for 2 hours, then strain through a sieve, bring to the boil and add:

1 medium sized carrot
cut in wafer thin
slices
1 large or two medium
sized potatoes diced

8 oz. shelled fresh
or frozen peas
2 tablespoons rice
1½ dozen Polpetti
(see page 40)

Allow to boil, not too quickly, for 20 minutes, and serve hot, handing grated Parmesan cheese to be added at will.

POLPETTI
Meat Balls
TO SERVE 4

1 lb. lean beef
  passed through
  mincer
2 eggs
2 tablespoons grated
  Parmesan — optional
chopped parsley

3 slices stale bread
  soaked in milk to
  cover it for 10 min-
  utes, and then
  squeezed dry in the
  hands
salt and pepper
1 clove garlic, crushed

Having soaked and squeezed the bread so that all liquid is out of it, mix with the meat, lightly beaten eggs and seasonings. Having floured your hands, take a little of the mixture between them, and roll into a ball about the size of half an egg. Flatten them slightly, and fry on both sides in hot olive oil; allow to drain for a few minutes before adding to the soup.

BROWN LENTIL SOUP
TO SERVE 4

8 oz. brown lentils
1 onion finely chopped
1 clove garlic crushed
1 heaped tablespoon
  finely chopped parsley

4 tablespoons olive oil
1 medium size tin
  tomatoes
salt and pepper to taste

The lentils for this soup are the khaki-coloured whole lentils, *not* the orange-coloured dried lentils which require longer soaking.

Cook the lentils in 2 quarts of boiling, slightly salted water for 1 hour; strain — but don't throw away the liquor — and set on one side. Replace liquor in saucepan, bring to the boil and add parsley, onion and garlic, and when boiling furiously add the oil and allow to boil fairly briskly for a further 10 minutes. Add strained tomatoes; replace lentils and boil gently for 20 minutes more. Serve very hot.

SPINACH SOUP (1)

TO SERVE 4

1 lb. spinach, weighed
  before cooking
2 tablespoons olive oil
1 clove garlic, crushed

2 tablespoons flour
2 pints water, or,
  better, chicken
  stock

Wash, cook and purée spinach. Heat oil in heavy pan, add crushed garlic and when brown remove. Blend in the flour, add puréed spinach and water; bring to boil and cook gently for 30 minutes. Serve with croûtons of toast and grated Parmesan.

SPINACH SOUP (2)

TO SERVE 4

1 lb. spinach, weighed
  before cooking
1 tablespoon flour
salt

1 oz. butter
2 pints meat stock
  or milk

Wash spinach in several waters, cook gently in the water adhering to its leaves after the final washing plus a small pinch of salt. Cook rather longer than usual, and reduce water until spinach is nearly dry, then pass through a sieve or food mill.

Meanwhile heat butter in pan, blend flour and slowly add milk or stock and bring to boil, slowly add spinach pureé, mix well and serve hot with snippets of toast.

A SLIGHTLY RICHER SPINACH SOUP

Proceed as directed in Spinach soup (1), but at the end of 30 minutes' cooking add the following mixture:

2 egg yolks, lightly beaten
2 tablespoons grated
  Parmesan

salt and pepper
  to taste

Blend together and stir into boiling soup, allowing eggs to curdle slightly and serve immediately.

CHESTNUT SOUP
TO SERVE 4

8 oz. chestnuts
2 pints stock, or mixed
  stock and water

1 bay leaf
1 slice lean ham
2 cloves

Score the chestnuts across the pointed end, and bake in a moderate oven 10 to 15 minutes, after which it should be simple to remove the outer and inner skins.

Peel and put to cook slowly with the water and ham and seasonings, for 40 minutes or slightly longer. Pass through a sieve or food mill and serve with snippets of fried bread.

ZUPPA PAVESE
TO SERVE 4

For this really nourishing 'meal in itself' soup, you need a quart of clear chicken broth, into which at the end of its cooking time, while still boiling, one egg at a time is thrown for each consumer, stirred rapidly while it 'poaches', and removed to its individual soup bowl while the other eggs are similarly treated.

ALTERNATIVE METHOD FOR ZUPPA PAVESE

If you do not mind your eggs very lightly poached, place a ½-inch slice of toasted French bread in each individual soup bowl, and on to it break an egg very carefully so as not to break the yolk. Over this pour the boiling soup, and serve immediately.

ZUPPA PARADISO

TO SERVE 6

This recipe, given in Rose L. Sorce's *La Cucina*, is just too good not to be included.

2 quarts good soup stock	4 eggs separated
4 tablespoons bread-crumbs	4 tablespoons grated Parmesan
nutmeg	pepper and salt

Bring soup to the boil, slowly add the following mixture, a spoonful at a time:

Beat the egg whites till stiff, add beaten yolks and beat till well blended, then add cheese and breadcrumbs.

Boil 5 to 8 minutes and serve.

STRACCIATELLA

One more soup with eggs

TO SERVE 4

2 eggs	2 teaspoons fine semolina
1 tablespoon grated Parmesan	1½ pints chicken broth

Beat eggs, and blend with semolina and cheese, add ½ pint cold broth, and beat well. Bring the remainder of the broth to the boil, and slowly add the egg mixture, beating with a fork or whisk; allow to cook slowly for 4 or 5 minutes before serving. The eggs will appear as little flakes or 'rags' in the soup.

VEGETABLE SOUP

TO SERVE 4

3 large onions
1 lb. ripe fresh toma-
toes
1 clove garlic crushed
2 tablespoons olive oil

2 outer stalks celery
1 large carrot — cooked
a few green peas or
French beans
1 quart hot water

Heat oil in heavy pan, chop vegetables and cook in oil till slightly brown; add hot water gradually and cook together for 30 minutes. Pass through a food mill or sieve before serving.

ZUPPA ALLA FOUBONNE

TO SERVE 4

2 large leeks
2 carrots
1 slice ham
1 quart meat stock

2 large onions
1 yellow turnip
1 oz. butter

Heat butter in heavy pan, and in it place chopped vegetables and ham and cook gently until lightly browned. Add stock and cook together 40 minutes. Pass through a sieve or food mill, replace on heat and boil for a further 5 minutes. Serve with snippets of toast and grated Parmesan.

LETTUCE SOUP

TO SERVE 4

2 heads of lettuce —
  preferably cos lettuce
1 tablespoon olive oil

1½ pints salted water
1 clove garlic, crushed
grated Parmesan
croûtons of bread

Wash lettuce, shred finely and boil until tender in boiling salted water. Heat oil in heavy pan, allow crushed garlic to cook for 3 minutes, remove garlic and add oil to swiftly boiling lettuce a few minutes before serving. Serve with snippets of bread, black pepper and with it hand a bowl of grated Parmesan.

MARROW SOUP ALLA NAPOLITANA

TO SERVE 4

1 medium sized vege-
  table marrow or 1 lb.
  zucchini (the tiny mar-
  rows about 4 inches
  or 5 inches in length)
1 tablespoon lard
salt and pepper to taste

4 eggs
4 tablespoons grated
  Parmesan
2 tablespoons chopped
  parsley
1 teaspoon chopped
  fresh basil if obtainable
2 slices toasted bread

Cut the marrow into slices, and having heated the lard in a stewpan, add marrow, pepper and salt, and when it has cooked a few minutes but before it has started to brown, add sufficient water to cover. Cover the pan and cook gently until the marrow is tender (about 20 minutes).

Beat the eggs, add the Parmesan, parsley and basil, and add to the marrow mixture. Mix well, keep hot for a few minutes, but do not allow to boil or the eggs will curdle.

Serve in warmed soup bowls with croûtons of toast.

GARLIC SOUP

TO SERVE 4

4 cloves garlic, crushed
1 quart clear stock
2 tablespoons chopped
   parsley

2 tablespoons olive oil
4 tablespoons grated
   Parmesan
croûtons of toast

Heat oil in stewpan and in it sauté garlic for 2 or 3 minutes, add stock and simmer for 30 minutes. Strain into soup tureen, adding parsley and cheese at moment of serving, with croûtons of toast.

CHEESE AND ONION SOUP

TO SERVE 4

3 large onions
1 teaspoon flour
salt and pepper

2 oz. butter
1 quart hot stock
grated Parmesan cheese

Use a heavy pan for this soup. Heat butter until it begins to brown, add onions thinly sliced, and sprinkled with flour, fry briskly, turning with a wooden spoon to make sure all are cooked until they are brown rather than gold coloured. Add heated stock little by little, stirring all the time, add salt to taste, and a generous helping of freshly ground black pepper, and allow to boil for 20 minutes with saucepan uncovered.

Pour into heavy earthenware tureen, covering the surface with a raft of ½-inch slices of stale bread or toast, over which sprinkle a thick layer of grated Parmesan, or a mixture of Parmesan and grated Gruyère cheese. Place in very hot oven so that cheese melts and turns golden. Serve immediately.

CHEESE AND ONION SOUP
Alternative method of serving

While your soup is cooking, toast 3 or 4 slices of French bread, and place in layers in a soup tureen, with a mixture of grated Parmesan and grated Gruyère cheese between each layer, and for added richness, a little butter.

When the soup has finished cooking, pass through a sieve, and pour over the layers of bread and cheese, and let it stand in a medium oven for 10 minutes before serving.

HARICOT BEAN SOUP
TO SERVE 4

8 oz. haricot beans — soaked in water over-night
1 clove garlic, crushed
3 pints water

1 tablespoon olive oil
pepper and salt to taste
4 heaped tablespoons chopped parsley

Cover the beans with water, bring to the boil and cook slowly for at least 3 hours.

Towards the end of the cooking time, heat the olive oil, and to it add the crushed garlic and parsley and cook together for 5 minutes.

Pass beans and the water in which they have cooked through a sieve or food mill, return to the saucepan, and stir in the garlic mixture. Serve hot with snippets of toast, and if liked, hand with the soup a dish of grated Parmesan.

CREAM OF TOMATO SOUP

TO SERVE 4

3 oz. butter
1 tablespoon flour
6 large tomatoes or
  1 medium sized tin
  of tomatoes
1 large or 2 small
  onions

1 tablespoon chopped
  parsley
1½ pints beef stock
1 gill cream
grated Parmesan
croûtons of bread
  toasted

Heat the butter in a heavy pan, and in it cook finely chopped onions until yellow, add flour and blend together, then add tomatoes, skinned and seeded if raw, strained if they are the tinned variety, and the chopped parsley. Season with salt and pepper and allow to cook over a slow heat, stirring all the time; after 3 or 4 minutes add stock, bring to boil and allow to cook gently for 30 minutes. Pass through sieve or food mill, re-heat, adding a little more stock if it seems too thick. Into a soup tureen place the cream and a knob of butter. Pour over this a little of the purée and beat with an egg whisk before adding the remainder. Serve garnished with croûtons and grated Parmesan.

CREAM OF MUSHROOM SOUP

1½ to 2 oz. butter	1½ pints hot milk
2 tablespoons flour	pepper and salt

Prepare a béchamel sauce as directed under cream soups (page 35). Keep hot in top of double boiler while preparing the following:

12 oz. mushrooms chopped finely	2 tablespoons sherry
	1 clove garlic
1 tablespoon chopped parsley	pepper and salt
	½ pint chicken stock
2 oz. butter	nutmeg, if liked

Heat the butter, and in it allow the crushed garlic to cook for a few minutes; remove, and add the mushrooms, cut small, and allow to sauté gently until cooked; add the wine and bring to a bubbling boil; reduce the heat, add the parsley and seasonings and cook gently for a few minutes before adding the stock. Bring to the boil before amalgamating with the béchamel, which should be keeping hot in the top of your double boiler. Serve very hot.

FISH SOUPS

In Southern France and in Italy fish soups are immensely popular, and for that reason, a few recipes ought rightly to appear in any compendium of Italian cooking.

Where your Italian cook says casually 'take a selection of fish', it has to be remembered that in his selection can be included a great many fish that are not native to our waters, nor easily obtainable in this country, such as octopus, lampreys (a variety of eel), calamari or squid, scampi. But we can still, given a little ingenuity, produce 'a selection of fish' that should produce a fish soup that is tasty and nourishing. Try combining sole with prawns or shrimps, a few scallops, a little smoked haddock, or smoked cod fillet — just let your imagination work and let your eye wander around the fishmonger's slab.

ZUPPA ALLA MARINARA

Sailors' soup

TO SERVE 4

about 2 lb. fish,
  including heads and tails
  and some shellfish
bay leaf
peppercorns
parsley
2 pints water

2 tablespoons white wine
1 small onion, chopped
1 stalk celery, chopped
4 tomatoes, peeled and
  chopped
1 oz. butter
salt and pepper

Chop fish in pieces. Make stock by combining heads, skins and a couple of pieces of the cheaper fish with bay leaf, peppercorns, parsley and water. Boil for about 20 minutes. Meanwhile melt the butter in a saucepan and sauté onion until golden brown, add celery, tomatoes and seasoning, sauté a few minutes longer, add wine. Strain stock, bring to boil and gently poach remainder of fish until cooked. Combine with onion, tomatoes, celery and wine and serve with snippets of toast or fried bread.

ZUPPA DI PESCE DEI PESCATORI DI POZZUOLI

Fish soup made by the fishermen of Pozzuoli

From Pozzuoli, once one of the chief commercial ports of the Mediterranean in the days of Roman domination, and previously one of the most important Greek cities of the region, and now not much more than a fishing village, the fishing fleet goes out each year for a fishing season in the waters of Santa Marinella. The villagers help the fishermen with their nets and it is the custom for the fishermen to prepare, at sea, a delicious fish soup, which they share with the villagers. This is a soup you won't be able to make at home, one you won't be able to taste, unless you happen one day to be lucky enough to join this fishing fleet during their summer migration from Pozzuoli to Santa Marinella. But imagine the scene, the rough old-fashioned stove on board the boat, the earthenware pot in which, with plenty of water, an assortment of freshly caught and cleaned fish is cooked, with a few tomatoes, a clove or two of garlic, a few spoonfuls of oil, and a coarsely chopped red pepper; cooked together for twenty minutes or so, then served in earthenware soup plates, with lumps of home-baked bread brought by the villagers to the fishing fleet.

ZUPPA DI PESCE ALLA GENOVESE

Genoese fish soup

TO SERVE 4

2 lb. assorted flat and shell fish, prepared and, in the case of the flat fish, cut in pieces; saving the heads, skins and bones to make stock by cooking with 2 pints of water, a bay leaf and a few peppercorns

2 tablespoons oil
1 or 2 stalks celery
1 bay leaf
2 tablespoons dry white wine
2 anchovies
1 clove garlic
1 medium sized onion
1 tablespoon chopped parsley
1 pint cleaned mussels

Heat the oil and in it brown the chopped onion, add the chopped celery and parsley, and the anchovies cut small, the crushed clove of garlic, strained fish stock and the wine and cook together 2 or 3 minutes; add the prepared fish, with the exception of the mussels, and cook together for 20 minutes; about 12 minutes before serving, add the cleaned mussels and continue to cook until all are opened, then serve the soup immediately, with slices of crisp toast or freshly fried bread.

ZUPPA DI PESCE ALLA SIRACUSANA

Fish soup as prepared in Syracuse

TO SERVE 4

Another fishing town, Syracuse, where carp swim lazily in the spring into which Arethusa is said to have changed when pursued by the river-god Alpheus, and where, later on, Nelson put in for a sufficiently long time to write one of his famous letters to Emma Hamilton before proceeding to his victory at the Nile. A famous fish soup is served in this pleasant Sicilian town.

2 lb. assorted fish, the heads, skins and bones of which are to be used to make 2 pints stock as in previous recipe	1 stalk celery
	2 tablespoons oil
	salt and pepper
	1 tablespoon chopped parsley
	1 bay leaf
1 medium sized onion	4 or 6 tomatoes
1 clove crushed garlic	1 gill white wine

This is a dish cooked in the oven. In a fireproof casserole large enough to hold the entire mixture, place your prepared fish, the larger pieces cut small, together with the chopped onion, parsley, bay leaf, celery cut small, tomatoes skinned and cut up, crushed garlic, oil, wine and sufficient of the fish stock to cover well. Season with salt and pepper, put the lid of the casserole on and weight it down if necessary to ensure a tight fit, and place in a moderate oven for 40 minutes. Before serving, remove the bay leaf. Serve with toasted or fried bread.

The Italian term *pasta* covers a multitude of various shapes and forms of what we tend to lump together in our minds under the heading of *macaroni* or *spaghetti*.

For centuries now *pasta* has formed an integral part of the Italian diet, but whether or not it originated in that country is open to question. One theory is that it was among the many curiosities and wonders brought back by the traveller Marco Polo when he returned to Italy during the thirteenth century after years of travel in the Orient, and in an account of his travels there is a description of the Chinese making a kind of dough which they cut in strips and dried in the sun, which strips he refers to by the Italian name of *lasagne*, the name used to this day in Italy for one of the broad, flat ribbon-type *pastas*.

Earlier than Marco Polo, however,

there is a reference to *pasta* in Italian literature, in the *Life of the Blessed Hermit William*, a holy man who lived around the year 1200, which rather discounts the Marco Polo legend.

It looks as though we are safe to assume that *macaroni* has as good a chance of being native to Italy as *noodles* have of being Chinese in origin; the name given to the kind of *pasta* matters less for the purpose of this book than the various ways of cooking the product.

A word first of all about the various types of *pasta* to be met with in Italy. Starting with the fine string-like *vermicelli*, too fine to have a bore through its centre, the tubular types come in all widths from the regular and familiar *macaroni* and *spaghetti*, to the 3-inch lengths of *cannelloni*, $\frac{3}{4}$ inch in diameter which, after a preliminary cooking in boiling water, are stuffed and re-cooked in various ways, and served up with sauce, or with cheese and butter.

There are the fancy shapes of *pasta*,

shells, elbows, cartwheels, twists, even alphabet letters, and there are the various flat types, the narrow *noodles*, the broader *tagliatellini*, progressing to the broad *lasagne*, and there are also the tiny rice-type grains known as *pastina*, and small star-shapes used as a garnish for soups. The variety is infinite and so are the possibilities of cooking the various types into tempting dishes.

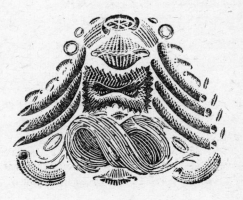

Cooking Procedures

Provided one remembers a few simple rules, nothing could be much simpler than the cooking of pasta.

1. See to it that you use a large utensil, a really capacious saucepan in which is an ample quantity of really boiling water — allow at least a gallon of boiling water per lb. of pasta, and to each gallon add a tablespoon of cooking salt. Before attempting to add the pasta, see that the water is at a proper boil, and add the pasta slowly so as not to let the water go off the boil, for once the temperature of the water drops below boiling point you are running the risk of having your pasta turn into a soft, rubbery mass, instead of the desired separate strands or pieces, depending on which variety of pasta you are cooking.

   If you are using the long, uncut spaghetti or macaroni, don't spoil the Italian appearance of your finished dish by breaking the pasta into shorter lengths; don't get alarmed if at first the long ends stick out of your saucepan of water; once the submerged part has been heated through it will soften sufficiently for you to be able to persuade the long ends to follow suit.

   One reason for the emphasis on using a large enough saucepan is the need to allow for the 'frothing' that takes place when once the pasta itself reaches boiling point; lower your heat a trifle when this occurs, but not sufficiently to let the water drop below boiling point. From time to time run a fork or spoon around your saucepan to loosen any stray ends of pasta that may adhere to the bottom or sides of the utensil.

2. Whatever you do, don't fall into the error of over-cooking your pasta, and where cooking time is concerned, you may have to go through a period of trial and error before you discover the correct cooking time for you own particular taste.

   The true Italian likes to be able to bite his cooked pasta: he will tell you it must be *al dente* (to suit the tooth), but while it must certainly not be soft enough to dissolve in the mouth, it must need only the tenderest of 'bites', such as you might give to — shall we say — a piece of Shrove Tuesday pancake. The cooking time will vary with the different varieties and thicknesses of pasta, and it is a fairly safe maxim in the early days of pasta-cooking to study the instructions given on the package of whichever type you choose, and to cook your pasta a minute or so less than the time suggested, then fish out a small piece and test it for yourself either by biting through it, or by pressing it between two fingers. A few experimental 'trial runs' will soon give you a guide to your own best cooking times. The following table will be helpful in a broad sense, but your own experience will eventually stand you in better stead.

3. TABLE OF COOKING TIMES
(Approximate only)

Ordinary spaghetti	8—12 minutes
Very thin spaghetti, vermicelli	6—10 minutes
Long macaroni	10—12 minutes
Macaroni shells, wagon wheels etc.	8—12 minutes
Broad noodles such as lasagne	6—9 minutes
Medium noodles — tagliatelle	4—6 minutes
Alphabet macaroni, pastina (the ricelike macaroni used in soup), small stars, etc.	5—7 minutes
Rigatoni or gavatoni (very large macaroni)	10—12 minutes

And remember, the home-made pasta needs usually no more than half the length of time to cook in comparison with the bought varieties.

4. To make sure that the cooked pasta will have no slimy outer covering, it is an excellent idea to 'blanch' it as soon as it is cooked by removing it from the heat, and before draining it through a colander, adding a cup of cold water to the boiling mass. Stir rapidly after the addition of cold water, then drain immediately through a colander, and, once drained, pile on a warm dish.

5. Having transferred your pasta to a warmed dish or bowl, add whatever sauce you have prepared and serve immediately, handing at the same time a bowl of grated Parmesan cheese, to be added to the taste of the consumer.

How Much Pasta Per Person?

It is difficult to suggest quantities of pasta per person, for while one pound of pasta might be ample for half a dozen people, there are addicts to whom a personal share of half a pound might not be too much, while others might abstain from tackling more than two ounces. A fairly 'safe' allowance is three ounces per person, plus an added three or four ounces for every sixth person, to allow for that little more an addict might demand.

The following recipes will give you an idea of some of the many ways you can serve this typically Italian food once you have mastered the simple art of preparing your pasta by its initial cooking in boiling water.

These all come under the category of *Pasta asciutta* (dry pasta) to distinguish them from *Pasta in Brodo*, or pasta served as an addition and an essential ingredient of certain broths and soups.

A RECIPE FOR HOME-MADE PASTA

Although there are excellent commercial brands of pasta in the various shapes and sizes, if you are a good pastry maker and have time to experiment, you may care to try your hand at making pasta for yourself. If you do, remember that the cooking time for the home-made variety is considerably less than that required for the packaged types — 5 to 7 minutes is all that is necessary.

You will need a fairly large pastry board, and a longer-than-usual rolling pin.

The following quantities will give you sufficient tagliatelle, the most usual type of home-made pasta, for 6 people.

1 lb. flour	a pinch of salt
2 or preferably 3 eggs	lukewarm water

Pile your flour in a mound on your pastry board, making a well in the middle into which break your eggs, adding salt, and to start with a couple of tablespoons of lukewarm water. Fold the flour over the eggs and water and knead until the liquid is used up. If the paste is too stiff, add a little more water, but be careful not to 'drown' it. When the paste can be formed into a fairly solid ball, its consistency is right. You should now knead it, flouring your hands lightly from time to time, and flouring the board, for at least 10 minutes; then, dividing it into 2 portions start the rolling process. It will need quite 10 rollings and the board and roller should be lightly floured between rollings. Finally it should be thin enough, metaphorically speaking, to read the newspaper through it. Spread a floured cloth over the back of a chair and lay the paste over it while you proceed similarly with the other half. When both sheets are rolled thin, leave them to dry out for 30 minutes, after which roll them up as you would a Swiss roll, or pinwheel biscuit mixture, and with a sharp knife cut across the roll at intervals of a quarter of an inch or less. Lay them on a floured cloth until you are ready to cook your tagliatelle, and remember, 5 to 7 minutes in boiling salted water will be ample.

A useful hint — if you have difficulty in finding a really long roller for pasta, a length of broomstick makes an excellent one, and for drying the pasta, again a length of broomstick resting on two chairbacks, so that the pasta can hang over a cloth draped over the broomstick, is a useful dodge to remember.

TAGLIATELLE ALLA CREMA

TO SERVE 6

1 lb. cooked tagliatelle
8 tablespoons grated
    Parmesan
2 tablespoons flour

3 eggs
4 oz. butter
pinch of nutmeg
pinch of salt
1 pint milk

Place 4 tablespoons of the grated cheese with the flour in a saucepan and mix slowly with the milk and a pinch of salt and nutmeg. Place on a slow heat and stir with a wooden spoon until it thickens, add a nut of butter and blend well, then remove from the fire, add the remainder of the butter and the balance of the grated cheese, and finally, when it has cooled a trifle, the beaten yolks of the 3 eggs. Whip the egg whites separately and fold into the first mixture. Add the cooked and drained tagliatelle to the sauce, place in a greased earthenware or oven-glass dish, and allow to cook in a medium oven for 15 minutes.

TAGLIATELLE WITH ANCHOVY AND TUNNY FISH

TO SERVE 4

12 oz. cooked tagliatelle
6 oz. tin of tunny
    fish
3 or 4 anchovies
½ pint good stock

salt and pepper
2 tablespoons olive oil
1 clove garlic
1 tablespoon freshly
    chopped parsley

Heat oil in a heavy pan, add garlic and cook for 2 or 3 minutes, add tunny and anchovies broken into small pieces or pounded, add parsley and cook for 4 or 5 minutes. Season with salt and pepper. Add stock slowly and bring to boiling point. Pour over cooked tagliatelle and mix well.

SOUFFLÉ OF TAGLIATELLE

TO SERVE 4

1 lb. tagliatelle	6 tablespoons grated
1½ teaspoons flour	Parmesan
3 oz. butter	salt and pepper
¾ pint milk	a pinch of nutmeg
4 eggs	

The home-made pasta made with eggs is preferable for this, though the commercially made tagliatelle may be used. Cook in boiling salted water in the approved manner, remembering that whereas the bought variety will need 10 to 12 minutes, the home-made will need no more than 5.

Meanwhile prepare the following sauce:

Melt butter in a saucepan, and before it begins to turn brown, blend in the flour and add milk slowly. Stir until it thickens and allow to cook over boiling water for a further 12 to 15 minutes, season with salt, pepper, nutmeg and the grated Parmesan, mix well and remove from the heat. Separate eggs, beat yolks lightly and add to the sauce when it has cooled a little, otherwise the yolks may curdle. Whip egg whites stiff and fold into the sauce. Have ready the cooked and drained tagliatelle, combine with the sauce, slowly, so as to ensure it is really well mixed. Place in a buttered soufflé dish and cook in moderate oven for 20 minutes. Serve in the dish in which it is cooked.

SPAGHETTI CON SALSA DI VONGOLE

Spaghetti with Clam Sauce

TO SERVE 6

1 lb. spaghetti cooked in the approved manner. When cooked and drained pour over it hot clam sauce (see page 221) and serve with or without grated Parmesan cheese.

FETTUCINE WITH MEAT SAUCE AND CHEESE
TO SERVE 4

Fettucine are our old friends, home-made tagliatelle, hiding, so to speak, under a pseudonym, the name given them in the district around Rome. For this dish you need the following ingredients:

1 lb. fettucine	½ pint or rather more
4 tablespoons grated	brown sauce
Parmesan	(see page 215)

When the fettucine are cooked and drained, place in a heated deep fireproof dish, and cover with the meat sauce and the grated Parmesan, lifting the fettucine with two forks to ensure that it is completely masked by the sauce. Serve with a bowl containing more grated Parmesan, to be added at will.

ELBOW MACARONI PIE
TO SERVE 4

12 oz. elbow macaroni	8 oz. cooked meat,
¾ pint tomato sauce	chopped finely
(see page 217)	2 eggs
4 tablespoons grated	short crust pastry suffi-
Parmesan cheese	cient to line and top
	your casserole

Grease an earthenware or oven-glass casserole and line with pastry. Mix together your cooked macaroni, tomato sauce, cheese and chopped meat and lay on top of pastry. Beat eggs lightly and pour over the mixture. Cover with short crust pastry, and bake in moderate oven for 30 minutes, or until crust is brown. Serve hot.

This with a simple salad makes a fairly sustaining meal.

SPAGHETTI WITH MEAT BALLS

TO SERVE 6

1 lb. spaghetti or ma-
caroni
1 small onion
1 or 2 cloves of garlic,
crushed
3 tablespoons olive oil
1 large tin tomatoes
1 tablespoon tomato paste
½ pint water
1 tablespoon brown sugar
a good pinch of orega-
no if available, or
failing this a pinch of
dried thyme

pepper and salt to taste

Meat Balls:

1 lb. lean beef passed
through the mincer
2 thick slices white
bread
1 small onion
1 tablespoon chopped
parsley
3 oz. grated Parmesan
1 egg
salt and pepper to taste

Soak the bread in water, squeeze dry and mash with a fork, and to it add the onion chopped finely, the parsley, minced beef, cheese and seasonings. Beat the egg lightly and combine with the foregoing mixture; shape into small balls — this amount should make about 12 — and fry in hot fat. Drain and set aside.

Heat the oil in a heavy pan, add chopped onion and crushed garlic and cook till golden; add strained tomatoes, tomato paste thinned down with a little water, the balance of the ½ pint water, sugar, oregano, pepper and salt; lower heat, cover and cook slowly for an hour.

At the end of an hour, add the meat balls, cover pan once more and allow to cook slowly for another 30 minutes before serving over the freshly cooked spaghetti.

With this dish hand a bowl of freshly grated Parmesan, to be added at will.

BAKED MACARONI WITH CHEESE

TO SERVE 4

1 pint milk	8 oz. elbow macaroni
salt and pepper to taste	8 oz. Cheddar cheese

Partly cook macaroni in boiling salted water — drain. Scald milk, stir in macaroni, add pepper and salt, grate and add cheese. When well blended, transfer to fireproof casserole and bake 30 minutes in moderate oven, stirring gently after about 10 minutes to make sure it is not sticking to bottom of casserole.

SPAGHETTI WITH BUTTER AND CHEESE

One of the simplest and at the same time one of the most delicious macaroni dishes this, and one for which any of the various forms of pasta may be employed.

For each person allow:

3 to 4 oz. pasta	1 really generous lump
1 tablespoon or more	of good butter
of grated Parmesan	
cheese	

The method of cooking pasta has already been described in detail on page 56.

When cooked, blanched and drained, stir the butter and cheese into the dish of pasta, allow to melt and serve immediately, handing at the same time a dish of the grated cheese so that more may be added at will.

BAKED MACARONI WITH SOUR CREAM

TO SERVE 4

8 oz. elbow macaroni	½ pint sour cream
12 oz. finely chopped cooked ham	4 eggs
	salt to taste

Cook and drain macaroni. Separate eggs. Beat yolks and to them add cream, salt and chopped ham. Add drained macaroni. Pile into buttered casserole. Whip egg whites stiffly and fold into mixture. Bake 30 minutes in moderate oven.

SPAGHETTI WITH HAM

For each person allow:

½ oz. butter	2 oz. ham, or better, if you can purchase it in your vicinity, the raw ham that is so popular in Italy
3 to 4 oz. spaghetti, tagliatelle, or any form of pasta particularly liked	

While your pasta is cooking in boiling salted water, cut your ham into long, thin strips and sauté in the butter in a heavy pan. When the pasta is blanched and drained, combine with the ham and serve immediately.

SPAGHETTI WITH OIL AND GARLIC

TO SERVE 2

8 oz. spaghetti
4 tablespoons best olive oil
at least 2 cloves garlic,
  crushed

a generous pinch of
  basil
salt and pepper to taste

While your spaghetti is cooking, heat the oil in a heavy pan, add crushed garlic and basil, and cook for 2 or 3 minutes so as to allow the oil to become thoroughly impregnated with the flavour of the garlic.

When the spaghetti has been cooked and drained, pile in a heated dish, add the oil and garlic mixture, blend well, and serve with freshly ground black pepper, salt and generous helpings of freshly ground Parmesan.

SPAGHETTI WITH GREEN OLIVE OIL SAUCE

TO SERVE 2

8 oz. spaghetti
4 tablespoons olive oil
grated Parmesan
black pepper

4 cloves garlic, chopped
  finely or crushed
at least 4 heaped table-
  spoons finely chopped
  parsley

Heat oil in a heavy pan; add garlic and allow to brown slightly, add chopped parsley and simmer gently for 5 minutes. Pour over cooked and drained spaghetti, mix well and serve with grated Parmesan and black pepper.

Three Typically Sicilian Recipes

SPAGHETTI WITH ANCHOVIES

TO SERVE 4

1 lb. spaghetti or
  'shells'
just under ¼ pint
  good olive oil
1 clove garlic

1 small tin anchovies
  (about a dozen fillets)
8 tablespoons grated
  Parmesan cheese
salt and pepper

Heat your oil in a heavy frying pan, and when hot add garlic, crushed, and fry until it is brown, then remove. Chop anchovies into short lengths, add to hot oil and cook for a couple of minutes, stirring with a wooden spoon. Add plenty of black pepper, but add salt with caution, remembering the saltiness of anchovies. Add this to a dish of cooked and drained spaghetti, topping with the grated Parmesan cheese, and serve immediately.

MACARONI WITH BROCCOLI

TO SERVE 4

1 lb. elbow macaroni
¼ pint olive oil
grated Parmesan

1 lb. young broccoli
salt

While the macaroni is cooking, clean the broccoli, break into small pieces, and cook 10 minutes in boiling salted water. Heat oil, in a heavy frying pan, drain and add broccoli, and fry lightly for 3 or 4 minutes.

Grease a casserole, sprinkle with grated Parmesan. Pile into this the cooked and drained macaroni, and over it pour the broccoli and oil. Mix well. Sprinkle with more grated Parmesan, and place in a hot oven for 5 minutes. Serve very hot.

SPAGHETTI WITH FRESH FENNEL SAUCE

TO SERVE 4 OR 5

1 lb. spaghetti	1 lb. fennel
4 tablespoons olive oil	1 large or 2 small onions
½ pint cold water	1 lb. fresh sardines,
6 oz. dried bread-	pilchards or sprats
crumbs	1 tablespoon sultanas
1 tablespoon pine nuts	or seedless raisins
or blanched almonds	salt and pepper

Clean and bone fish. Clean fennel and cook for 15 minutes in about a quart of boiling water. Drain and chop small. Heat olive oil in a stewpan and cook in it the chopped onion until it is a golden colour, add fish, cook gently for 10 minutes, stirring frequently; add fennel, sultanas and nuts, cold water and seasoning and allow to simmer gently for 10 minutes. Place breadcrumbs on a fireproof plate below a hot grill for a few seconds to brown.

Meanwhile cook the spaghetti in the approved method. When cooked and drained, place in deep, warmed dish, pour over half the fish and fennel sauce and half the breadcrumbs and mix well. Then pile on balance of fennel mixture and top with remainder of breadcrumbs and serve very hot.

SPAGHETTI WITH BACON, EGG, AND ONION

TO SERVE 4

3 to 4 oz. spaghetti	4 rashers back bacon
per person	4 eggs
oil or butter for frying	4 medium sized onions

While you are cooking your spaghetti in the approved manner, peel and chop your onions finely and fry them to a light golden hue in a heavy frying pan with olive oil or butter; when they are evenly coloured a pale gold, add your rashers cut into small pieces. By the time these are cooked your spaghetti should be ready for blanching and draining. When drained, add it to the bacon and onion in the pan, break the eggs on to the mixture, stir rapidly with a wooden spoon, and serve immediately the eggs have begun to thicken, a matter of a few seconds. Freshly ground black pepper is a necessary adjunct to this dish, as is a dish of freshly grated Parmesan cheese to be handed to the consumers and added to individual taste.

LASAGNE VERDI

These are the pale green strips of pasta, cut in oblongs as large as 3 inches by 2 inches, and although it is possible and permissible to use in their place the green ribbon noodles obtainable in most shops that sell pasta, you may, if you are successful with your home-made tagliatelle, wish to experiment with this refinement of pasta.

For 6 people the quantities are the same as those for tagliatelle (see page 58), except that instead of lukewarm water for mixing, you need 3 oz. puréed spinach (which is weighed after, not before cooking, remember).

Start again with 1 lb. of flour heaped on a board, with a well made in the centre into which you break 3 eggs. After blending these with the flour, work in the spinach, and proceed with your kneading, rolling, drying and cutting as you did for the tagliatelle, except that instead of cutting the pasta into strips, you cut it into rather large, flat oblongs.

Using either your home-made oblongs of lasagne or bought green noodles, you can make one of the most famous pasta dishes of all:

LASAGNE AL FORNO

TO SERVE 6

1 lb. lasagne	1 tablespoon tomato
2 tablespoons olive oil	paste
1 lb. minced beef	1 lb. lasagne or green
1 medium sized onion,	noodles
chopped finely	12 oz. to 1 lb. Mozzarella
1 crushed clove of garlic	or Bel Paese cheese
1 pint water	3 tablespoons grated
salt and pepper	Parmesan

Heat oil in a heavy frying pan, add the onion and garlic, and when slightly browned, add and brown the minced meat. Blend the tomato paste with a little water, pepper and salt, dilute with the balance of the water and pour slowly over the meat; cover and allow to simmer gently for 1½ hours.

Cook lasagne in rapidly boiling salted water, 5 to 7 minutes if the lasagne is home-made, 15 minutes if commercially packaged. Blanch and drain.

Grease an oven glass or earthenware casserole, and in it lay a layer of the cooked lasagne, a layer of meat sauce and a layer of Mozzarella or failing this of Bel Paese. Continue filling the dish in layers until all the ingredients are used up, finishing with the balance of the sauce poured over the finished dish, which should be topped with grated Parmesan. Bake for 20 minutes in medium oven.

LASAGNE IMBOTTITE
Stuffed Noodles

TO SERVE 4

2 tablespoons olive oil
1 medium sized tin
    tomatoes
4 tablespoons hot water
1 clove garlic, crushed
salt and pepper to taste
6 tablespoons grated
    Parmesan

1 tablespoon tomato paste
1 stick celery, cut small
12 oz. cottage cheese
8 oz. Bel Paese
8 oz. sausages
12 oz. home-made
    lasagne or green
    bought noodles

Heat olive oil in heavy pan and brown garlic for about 3 minutes; blend the tomato paste with hot water, and add to garlic, together with diced celery and tomatoes; after about 3 minutes, lower heat and allow to simmer for 1 hour. Season with pepper and salt.

Fry sausage in separate pan until brown, and cut into small pieces.

Boil lasagne or noodles in boiling salted water as previously directed. Drain.

Into a greased casserole place alternate layers of lasagne, tomato sauce, Parmesan, more sauce, Bel Paese, sausage and more sauce, finishing with a layer of sauce topped with grated cheese. Bake in moderate oven 20 minutes. When serving hand at the same time balance of tomato sauce and grated Parmesan.

CANNELLONI FILLED WITH CHEESE AND SAUSAGE

TO SERVE 4

Although it is possible to buy the large 'channel' macaroni, and after a preliminary cooking to fill them with the filling mixture, the home-made variety is far preferable, and once again the recipe for pasta (page 58) may be used. But when it has had its final rolling it must be cut into oblongs about 4 inches by 3 inches, and cooked, a few at a time, in boiling salted water for 4 or 5 minutes, removed gently with a perforated spoon so as not to break them, and allowed to cool. For 4 people allow 20 to 24 cannelloni.

Filling:

12 oz. cottage cheese
grated Parmesan

8 oz. sausages
¼ pint tomato sauce
(see page 217)

Prick the sausages and place them in a pan, cover with water, heat and allow to cook until the water has evaporated, then let the sausages remain a few minutes in the fat that will have escaped from them in the cooking. Cool slightly, skin and mash the filling and mix with the cheese.

Place a little filling, about a tablespoon, in the centre of each piece of pasta, and roll up into a tube. Grease a flat fireproof dish well and in it place the cannelloni side by side, and over them pour tomato sauce, not quite sufficient to cover them; dot with butter and sprinkle with grated Parmesan cheese, and place in moderate oven for 15 minutes before serving.

Ravioli and Gnocchi

Having mastered the cooking of pasta of the macaroni and spaghetti variety, let us now proceed to the more involved types known broadly as *ravioli* and *gnocchi*.

Both may be made at home, and after a little practice made well, and although it is possible to purchase both types ready-made and needing only to be heated and added to a sauce, if there is time available to make one's own ravioli or gnocchi, the results are well worth while. Ravioli is the term loosely applied to the several varieties of little envelopes of paste filled with various forms of stuffing, and served either, like *pasta asciutta*, with a tomato or meat sauce, or, like *pasta in brodo*, in a clear consommé rather after the style of the Jewish *kraplech*, or the Chinese *pork pellets*.

Once you have become expert in the art of making tagliatelle at home, you may, if you wish, use the same recipe for your ravioli, agnolotti, anolini, tortellini, or cappelletti, to give a few of the various names given to the many types of filled pasta. But when your paste has been rolled as thin as possible (remember, thin enough for you to be able to read the newspaper — or at least the headlines — through it), instead of rolling it into a roll as you have done when making tagliatelle, keep it in two large, flat sheets, or, supposing your pastry board is on the small size, a greater number of small sheets of thin pasta.

As each sheet is rolled to the desired thinness, spread it on a clean cloth, and keep it covered with another cloth, so as to prevent its going crusty and becoming too breakable to handle.

When your paste is made and the filling you intend using is prepared, spread a sheet of the paste on to a floured pastry board, and dot with the filling at regular intervals, say a teaspoon of filling at intervals of about $1\frac{1}{2}$ to 2 inches. Cover lightly with the second sheet of paste, after having brushed the 'walks' between the lines of filling with beaten egg to ensure that the second sheet of paste will close down over the filling. You may then either use a small round cutter, or, less wastefully, run a pastry wheel between the fillings so that you have a series of little filled envelopes of paste. Transfer these to a floured dish, being careful not to let them overlap, and cover with a floured cloth or paper until you are ready to cook them.

These can be made overnight if wished.

To cook, have ready a large pan of boiling salted water and transfer your envelopes of pasta one at a time, until all are in the water, allowing them to cook for 4 or 5 minutes or until they rise to the top of the pan. Remove them one at a time with a perforated spoon or slice, place in a heated dish, and serve with a generous helping of melted butter and grated Parmesan, or with any preferred sauce. These little filled envelopes are equally delicious served in a clear consommé, as one more form of pasta in brodo. Another and slightly richer paste for ravioli and its kindred pastas can be made as follows:

12 oz. flour
2 eggs
1 oz. butter
½ pint or slightly less warm water
pinch salt

Sift flour and salt together. Place on a board and make a well into which break the eggs. When you have kneaded them into the flour, add the softened butter, and gradually sufficient lukewarm water to make a dough. Knead until smooth and easy to handle; cover and allow to stand for 10 to 15 minutes before dividing into two portions and rolling very thin on a lightly floured board, remembering to flour the paste lightly between each of its several rollings.

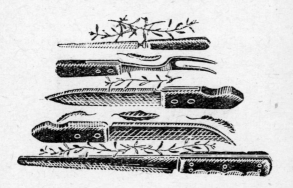

FILLINGS FOR RAVIOLI

Spinach filling

TO SERVE 6

8 oz. each cooked puréed spinach and chopped chicken or veal (cooked)	2 eggs
	½ clove garlic, if liked – crushed
2 oz. breadcrumbs	1 heaped tablespoon finely chopped parsley
4 tablespoons grated Parmesan cheese	salt and freshly ground black pepper

Mix dry ingredients and blend together with lightly beaten eggs. Drop in teaspoonfuls at regular intervals on one sheet of pasta, cover with second sheet and press together gently around each mound of filling. Cut into squares with pastry cutter, and cook in boiling salted water in deep saucepan for 5 or 6 minutes, or until the envelopes of pasta rise to the top of the boiling water. Transfer carefully with perforated spoon to a hot dish, serve with tomato sauce (see page 217) and when serving hand a bowl of freshly grated Parmesan cheese.

CHEESE FILLING

TO SERVE 6

5 oz. each grated Parmesan and Gruyère	pepper, salt, a pinch of nutmeg, and a pinch (fairly generous) of thyme
½ pint milk	
2 eggs	

Blend well together, place in spoonfuls on a sheet of pasta as directed for previous recipe, cover with second sheet, press down, cut with pastry cutter and cook in boiling, salted water as previously directed.

When dished up, serve with melted butter and hand additional grated Parmesan to be added at will.

CREAM CHEESE FILLING

TO SERVE 6

1 lb. cottage cheese
4 oz. grated Parmesan
1 whole egg and one
  egg yolk

2 tablespoons finely
  chopped parsley
freshly grated black
  pepper, salt and
  a pinch of nutmeg

Blend well together and use as a filling for ravioli.
  Serve with melted butter.

MEAT FILLING

TO SERVE 6

8 oz. each raw minced
  beef and raw minced
  veal
2 tablespoons olive oil
1 oz. grated Parmesan
1 tablespoon finely
  chopped parsley

1 egg
1 gill cooking
  sherry, or preferably
  Marsala
pepper and salt to taste
a clove of crushed
  garlic if liked

Heat oil in a heavy pan, add garlic (if you are using), and
chopped meat, and allow to cook for 5 or 6 minutes, add
the wine, and cook for another 20 minutes; cool, and then
add the beaten egg, Parmesan and seasonings; blend well,
and use as a filling for ravioli, or for cappelletti (little hats),
which latter are 2½-inch rounds of ravioli paste, in the centre
of which is placed a teaspoon of filling, after which the paste
is folded over and sealed at the edges with a fork.

CHICKEN FILLING

TO SERVE 4

4 oz. finely chopped cold
boiled chicken
4 oz. finely chopped cold
cooked veal or pork
8 oz. spinach, cooked
and puréed
4 tablespoons bread-
crumbs

2 tablespoons grated
Parmesan
1 egg
½ clove crushed garlic,
if liked
salt and pepper to taste
and a dash of nutmeg

Mix dry ingredients together, blend with the beaten egg and
use as a filling for ravioli.

CAPPELLETTI IN BRODO

'*Little hats in soup*'

Make cappelletti as described under Meat filling on page 79,
heat clear chicken broth to boiling point, drop in your 'little
hats', and allow to cook for 5 to 7 minutes before serving.

BACON AND SAUSAGE FILLING

TO SERVE 6

6 rashers lean bacon
8 oz. Mortadella
1 egg

pepper and salt
a pinch of nutmeg

Pass chopped bacon and sausage twice through mincer,
blend with beaten egg, add seasonings and use to fill ravioli
or cappelletti. This is an excellent filling for yet one more
variety of pasta in brodo when cooked for 5 or 6 minutes in
boiling clear soup.

Gnocchi

Although gnocchi is placed at the end of the various forms of pasta, it is about the easiest form to make at home, for it requires neither rolling nor filling and consists merely of little rolls, croquettes or circles of pasta, various recipes for which follow.

POTATO GNOCCHI
TO SERVE 4

2 lb. raw potatoes
8 oz. flour
2 eggs

½ oz. butter
salt and pepper to taste

Boil potatoes in salted water for 20 minutes, drain and mash with the butter; gradually incorporate the flour and beaten eggs and seasoning. Roll between floured hands into rolls the thickness of your finger and cut into pieces an inch long or slightly less. Have ready a pan of boiling salted water, and drop the gnocchi gently into the pan one by one, boiling for 3 or 4 minutes until they rise to the top — the water should boil only gently, not furiously. Transfer when cooked in a perforated spoon on to a heated greased fireproof dish, dot with butter and place in a warm oven long enough to allow the butter to melt. Serve plain, or with a meat or tomato sauce (see under *Sauces*, pages 213—34).

SEMOLINA GNOCCHI

TO SERVE 6

1¼ pints milk	8 oz. semolina
2 egg yolks	1½ oz. butter
3 or 4 oz. grated Parmesan	a pinch of nutmeg

Heat milk, and add semolina slowly, stirring constantly and cooking slowly until thick. Remove from fire, add beaten yolks of eggs, grated cheese and butter and seasonings and mix well. Rinse a flat dish with cold water and on it spread the semolina to a thickness of a ½ inch. Leave for an hour, and when cold, cut with a knife rinsed under the tap, into squares or diamonds 1½ inches or 2 inches across.

GNOCCHI ALLA ROMANA

Having prepared your gnocchi as above, butter a fireproof dish and in it lay a layer of gnocchi, sprinkling with grated Parmesan and dotting with butter. Add a second and a third layer, with Parmesan and dots of butter between each, and to make dish attractive pile your layers in pyramid form. When the last of the gnocchi are used up, sprinkle with more Parmesan and over the whole pour 1½ oz. melted butter. Place dish in moderate oven for 20 minutes or until the gnocchi have taken on a golden colour. Serve in the dish in which they were cooked.

GNOCCHI WITH TOMATO SAUCE

As an alternative to the above dish, make your gnocchi about one quarter the size, and serve hot with tomato sauce just sufficient to surround each dumpling with sauce but not to have the dish 'swimming' in sauce. With these, hand a bowl of grated Parmesan cheese.

Rice

Although pasta, either *pasta asciut-ta* (pasta eaten with some form of sauce) or *pasta in brodo* (pasta in soup) appears with fair regularity in the Italian daily diet all over the peninsula, there is, in the north, a tendency to vary this by the use of rice dishes. Rice is cultivated in northern Italy on a heavy scale, and that grown in the Piedmont area, that is to say the stretch of country lying between the Bay of Genoa on the South and the Grain Alps of Switzerland on the North, produces a particularly fine, hard grain, equal in quality to the best that Patna in India can offer, and ideally suited to the long, slow cooking that is a feature of Italian rice dishes.

It is as well to remember to ask for Piedmont rice, or failing this to specify Patna rice, as the shorter, rounder grained rice, known to my local grocer as 'pudding rice', though excellent for sweet rice pudding, is apt to produce a somewhat sticky risotto. If, when shopping at a small local shop, you are asked, as I have been asked: 'Do you want the pudding rice or *the other kind*?' it's fairly safe to plump for *the other kind*.

If you have never previously tried to cook a risotto, the instructions may come as a slight bombshell, but I promise you, if you will follow them faithfully, the result will surpass anything you might achieve if you were to give in to the temptation to 'par-boil the rice first of all', to mention but one of the many incorrect methods. To all such suggestions I cannot too emphatically say *don't*. Supposing you are about to produce a risotto for four people, start operations a good three-quarters of an hour before the meal is scheduled — and just supposing you happen to be a working housewife, let me assure you that, heretical though the suggestion may appear to be, an excellent risotto can be prepared in the morning before you leave for the day's work, and re-heated so as to produce a really good dish for dinner the same evening — moreover, the flavour is apt to be all the richer if the various ingredients have had all day in which to insinuate their many and varied flavours into the finished dish. The one ingredient I prefer not to allow to remain all day in the risotto is the portion of chopped mushrooms, which, to my way of thinking, are much better sautéed in butter or oil and added to the dish not more than twenty minutes before serving time.

One thing to remember where the use of rice in Italy is concerned is that except in the case of the famous Ossobucho, rice is not served with meats but whatever meat is used is mixed with the rice to form an integrated dish.

And now to your first risotto for four people.

PLAIN RISOTTO

TO SERVE 4

12 to 15 tablespoons Piedmont or Patna rice, the quantity depending on the appetites of the consumers

2 tablespoons best olive oil, or a mixture of oil and butter or, if you want it in the truly Milanese style, 2 oz. butter

2 medium sized onions chopped small

1½ pints or thereabouts of stock, chicken for preference, and if you want a touch of luxury, substitute 1 gill white wine for an equal quantity of stock

saffron for colouring

Heat the oil or butter in a heavy pan, add the onion, chopped small, and allow to cook until it is a golden yellow but *not* brown. Add the rice *dry*, and cook slowly together for a few minutes, stirring with a wooden spoon, until the grains are almost transparent. Now begin adding your stock — and now is a good moment to insert an asbestos mat between the pan and the direct heat of the stove. The stock is added in very small quantities a few tablespoons at a time, and the Risotto is stirred frequently to prevent sticking. When the first instalment of the stock is absorbed, add the next and so on until the rice has finished cooking, and most if not all of the stock has been used. This should take from 25 to 30 minutes. Test the rice for tenderness towards the end of this time, and when it is tender and the dish looks creamy but is not sticky, the risotto is ready for the table. The grains, though tender, should still be separate.

To give your risotto a truly Milanese appearance it should be coloured a primrose yellow (rather than a buttercup yellow) with saffron at the end of the cooking time. If you are using the filaments — the dried stamens of the autumn crocus — take 2 or 3 of these, and having pounded them to a powder and allowed them to steep 5 minutes or so in a little warmed stock, strain and add them to the rice. You may, however, have purchased a thimbleful of already powdered saffron from an Italian provision shop, in which case add it, small pinch by small pinch, until the desired colour is obtained, but be careful not to overdo the pinches, as a little goes a long way.

This dish, omitting the white wine, is excellent with nothing added but a generous lump of butter and a few tablespoons of grated Parmesan, stirred in, allowed to melt and served immediately, before it has a chance to go stringy. With it hand more grated Parmesan to be added at will, and more butter, and you have a truly classic Risotto *alla Milanese*.

PLAIN RISOTTO

A somewhat richer version

Proceed as before, but with the addition of white wine, and if you can procure about 1 oz. marrow from marrow bones, you will have a really rich dish.

You may also substitute Marsala for the white wine, but in this case I would advise against the marrow, as that and the Marsala combined would make the dish overrich for most palates.

Now for the variations of this simple and typically Italian dish:

MY OWN FAVOURITE RISOTTO

TO SERVE 4

12 tablespoons Piedmont rice
4 oz. butter
2 medium sized onions chopped small
1½ pints stock
4 oz. mushrooms chopped fine
8 oz. lean ham or gammon, cut into small pieces

8 oz. shelled cooked (or frozen) green peas
a few cooked French beans, if available
1 or 2 tomatoes, peeled and cut small
pepper and salt
a pinch of thyme
a pinch of nutmeg

Proceed as for plain risotto, but half-way through the cooking time add the mushrooms, which have been sautéed in butter, the ham, peas, beans and tomatoes, and the seasonings.

When serving, hand a bowl of freshly grated Parmesan, to be added at will.

MUSHROOM RISOTTO

TO SERVE 2

1 rasher streaky bacon
2 oz. butter
2 medium sized onions
6 oz. rice
12 oz. mushrooms
¾ pint stock

6 medium sized toma-
  toes
pepper, salt, nutmeg
4 to 6 oz. cold, lean meat
1 tablespoon sultanas

Cut the bacon small and fry lightly in the butter, remove from pan, and add to the pan the chopped onions, frying them for 2 or 3 minutes. Add the rice and cook gently until it is transparent — about 5 minutes — add all the mushrooms except about 2 tablespoons of chopped mushrooms which will be useful for garnishing; add sliced and peeled tomatoes, pepper, salt and a little grated nutmeg and replace bacon in pan. Add the stock in small instalments, giving the risotto a stir from time to time to prevent the rice sticking to the bottom of the pan. 10 minutes before serving, add the cold meat chopped small, and the sultanas, together with the remainder of the mushrooms which have been cut in small pieces and sautéed in a little butter. The rice should be cooked in about 30 minutes from the time it was added to the dish. Serve with grated Parmesan if liked.

RISOTTO WITH SHELLFISH

TO SERVE 4

Make a perfectly plain risotto, but instead of stock made from meat or chicken, use fish stock if available, or failing this, plain water plus 1 gill white wine.

Meanwhile, allowing 5 or 6 scampi or Dublin Bay prawns, or the equivalent quantity of lobster or peeled shrimps per person, sauté the shelled and cut up fish in a little butter to which a little crushed garlic has been added. Towards the end of the cooking of the risotto add the fish, together with the butter in which it has been cooked. Finally stir in butter and grated Parmesan.

RISOTTO WITH BRAINS

TO SERVE 4

12 oz. lean veal
a little beef marrow, if available
12 tablespoons Piedmont rice
4 oz. butter
1½ pints stock

saffron to colour
1 calf's brain
1 medium sized onion
1 tablespoon parsley
pepper and salt to taste
4 tablespoons grated Parmesan

Wash the brains in salt and water, remove the skin and fibres and let them remain in salt and water till ready to use.

Heat butter in a heavy pan, add chopped onion and allow to cook a few minutes until the onion is golden yellow, add the chopped parsley, chopped veal and marrow if available, and allow to brown for 8 to 10 minutes; add the rice and the stock little by little. Drain the brains and cut into small pieces, and when the dish has been cooking for 15 or 20 minutes add these to the risotto and continue cooking until the rice is tender. Just before serving, add the seasonings and the grated Parmesan.

CHICKEN RISOTTO

TO SERVE 4

If you have some left-over boiled chicken, remove any skin, and cut the meat into small pieces. You should have at least 1 lb. In addition you will need:

1 medium sized onion	2 peeled tomatoes
1 clove garlic, crushed	1 small carrot
4 oz. mushrooms	1 stalk celery
¼ pint chicken stock; and later, when rice added, 1 pint more	2 tablespoons or there-abouts of chopped lean ham or gammon
1 oz. butter	1 gill white wine
chopped parsley	pepper and salt
	12 oz. rice

Heat the butter and in it sauté the chopped onion, garlic, celery and chopped carrot; after 5 minutes add the chopped mushrooms, and the tomatoes cut small; allow to cook together for a couple of minutes, then stir in the chopped chicken, chopped ham and the wine and increase the heat so that the dish cooks fast for a couple of minutes more; add the seasonings; stir in the stock, cover the pan and allow to cook slowly for 30 minutes or so before adding the rice. Proceed as for an ordinary risotto, using chicken stock or water for further moistening during the cooking of the rice.

Finally stir in grated Parmesan and a generous portion of butter.

RISOTTO GENOVESE

Rice in the Genoese style

TO SERVE 4

For this dish the rice is first of all parboiled. Cook 12 oz. of rice in boiling, salted water in a large pan as previously directed, but remove and drain a few minutes before it is completely cooked, and when drained, turn it into a clean saucepan, and to it add the following sauce, plus a generous lump of butter, cooking together and stirring to avoid sticking, for 5 minutes or until the rice has finished cooking.

When serving, hand with the dish a bowlful of freshly grated Parmesan cheese.

SAUCE

8 oz. raw lean meat, beef or veal for preference, minced	2 or 3 carrots, washed and diced
2 or 3 stalks of celery, washed and cut fine	1 medium onion, chopped
pepper and salt to taste	chopped parsley
butter for frying the vegetables and meat	a pinch of oregano or thyme
	¼ pint white wine

Heat the butter, and in it sauté the vegetables until they are a golden colour; add the meat and allow to brown, stirring so as to prevent sticking. Add the wine, and cook fairly rapidly until the liquid has diminished by half, then cover and simmer for 1 hour, by which time the sauce should have the consistency of syrup.

RICE WITH TURNIPS

Riso e rape

TO SERVE 6

12 oz. peeled turnips
1 lb. rice
¼ pint tomato sauce
(see page 217)

butter for frying
2½ to 3 pints meat stock
salt and pepper to taste

Cut the turnips in slices, spread on a plate, sprinkle with salt, cover with another plate and allow to stand for 2 hours, so as to draw off the surplus water from the vegetables. At the end of this time, drain the turnips, and place in a heavy pan in which you have heated the butter; allow to brown a little, stirring with a wooden spoon so that they do not stick to the bottom of the pan; stir in the tomato sauce and allow to cook for 4 or 5 minutes, then cover with heated stock, bring to the boil and add the rice. Cook gently for 15 or 20 minutes, adding more stock if the dish begins to appear dry. Do not overcook, or the flavour is diminished.

RICE WITH CABBAGE

Riso e cavoli

TO SERVE 6

sufficient good hard
cabbage to weigh
12 oz. when the outside
leaves and hard
centre stalk have
been removed

1 lb. rice
2½ to 3 pints stock,
chicken stock for pre-
ference
salt and pepper to taste

Having removed the outer leaves and centre stalk of the cabbage, wash carefully, strain, and cut finely. Bring stock to the boil, add the cabbage, let it cook gently for 5 minutes, then add the rice and cook gently for a further 15 or 20 minutes, or until *al dente* (see page 56). To give a richer flavour to this, try the addition of 2 or 3 slices of lean ham, finely chopped, and a little tomato paste 'broken down' with a few tablespoons of the hot broth.

RICE AND PEAS AS SERVED IN VENICE

'Risi e bisi'

TO SERVE 6

3 lb. peas weighed be-
fore shelling
1 lb. rice
2½ to 3 pints hot meat
stock
1 tablespoon olive oil

1 tablespoon butter
1 tablespoon lard
2 tablespoons finely
chopped parsley
2 spring onions

Shell and wash peas. Heat oil, butter and lard in heavy pan, add finely chopped onions and parsley and cook gently. Add peas and allow to cook long enough to absorb fat. Then add just enough hot meat stock to cover and allow to bubble before adding rice, having done which, add a further ¼ pint heated stock and cook gently without stirring for 25 or 30 minutes until rice is cooked. At end of cooking stir in a further tablespoon of butter and 2 tablespoons of grated Parmesan, and when serving, hand a dish of grated Parmesan so that more may be added if wished. This dish should not be allowed to become too dry in the cooking.

BOILED RICE WITH BUTTER AND CHEESE

Riso in cagnoni

Allow 4 oz. rice per person. Cook the rice as directed above, and when it has finished cooking and has been strained, place in a heated casserole, and add generous portions of butter and grated Parmesan, mixing well before serving. As a variation, you may, if you wish, heat the butter first until it has become a golden liquid, and you may also, if you wish, flavour it with a little finely chopped garlic.

A simple dish by no means to be despised.

TO BOIL RICE
Now for a few comments on plain boiled rice.

You will need a large saucepan, with plenty of boiling water, and 1 or 1½ tablespoons of rice per person. The saucepan must be large enough for the rice to move about freely while it is cooking, which allows surplus starch to escape into the boiling water, which is something it cannot do under crowded conditions.

Some cooks prefer to wash the rice before cooking, but actually, so long as it is looked over and any remaining husks removed, washing is not necessary as any dust there may be in the rice will rise to the top during the cooking and is easily skimmed off. However, if you are going to feel better about washed rice, by all means wash it.

When the water is boiling rapidly and salt has been added, add the rice and allow it to boil fast from 15 to 20 minutes, depending on the quality of the rice and on personal taste. Towards the end of 15 minutes test a few grains by biting, and when they are soft, and before they have had a chance to become 'mushy', remove the saucepan from the stove, and strain the rice through a fairly fine colander. Run cold water through the colander, shaking the rice as you do so to remove any starch still adhering, and then place the rice in a lidless, heated fireproof dish in a warm — *not hot* — oven with the oven door left open, for a few minutes to dry. Alternatively, the drying can be achieved by placing the dish over a saucepan of boiling water on top of the stove for a minute or two.

RICE WITH CELERY
Riso e sedano

An agreeable dish is obtained by substituting for cabbage in the foregoing recipe a good head of celery, washed and chopped finely.

RICHER WAY OF SERVING BOILED RICE

Risotto in cagnoni di magro

TO SERVE 4

Cook 1 lb. rice in the approved fashion and when it has been cooked and drained, stir into it the following sauce:

1 onion chopped fine	1 tablespoon chopped
6 anchovies	parsley
4 tablespoons oil	¼ pint tomato sauce
	(see page 217)

Cook onion in the heated oil till yellow, stir in the parsley, and the anchovies, boned and cut into small pieces; cook together for 5 minutes, stir in tomato sauce, bring to boil and mix with the rice.

ARANGINI

TO SERVE 4

Often when a train has stopped at a small station in Italy or Sicily, the attendant wheeling the *Tavola Calda*, the trolley containing hot food to be consumed on the train, makes his way down the platform to the accompaniment of the cry *Aran-g-e-e-e-e-ni*, and the hardy traveller who takes a chance on this typically Italian tit-bit is handed a piece of brown paper, containing a warm mound of rice, the colour of a pale orange, the best way of eating which is out of the paper, using the paper later as a napkin to wipe mouth and hands.

To make 8 of these 'delicacies', you will need the following ingredients:

1 lb. rice	2 tablespoons chopped
4 tablespoons grated	parsley
Parmesan	2 hard-boiled eggs
1 beaten egg	(a refinement, this
1 tablespoon olive oil	addition)
a pinch of salt	breadcrumbs and oil
12 oz. lean minced beef	for deep frying

Cook the rice in boiling, salted water, drain and mix with half the beaten egg. Heat the olive oil in a heavy pan, brown the minced meat in this, remove from the heat and mix with grated cheese, parsley and chopped hard-boiled eggs.

Rinse the hands in cold water, take a handful of cooked rice, and in the centre of this place a generous portion of the foregoing mixture, closing the rice up to encase the mixture and form a ball. Repeat this until all the rice and all the filling is used up. Dip the balls in the balance of the beaten egg, coat with fine breadcrumbs and fry in deep, hot oil until they have taken on a light golden-brown colour.

A few left-over cooked spring peas are a welcome addition to the other ingredients.

The above recipe makes a delicious dish for home consumption, and is good eaten with hot tomato sauce, using any of the recipes under *Sauces*. The railway station variety is rather less luxurious, and the hard-boiled eggs are usually conspicuous by their absence, but nevertheless, it is tasty and filling on a long journey when there is no restaurant car on the train.

CHEESE RICE BALLS

TO SERVE 4

8 oz. left-over plain boiled rice	2 or three slices lean ham, cut into strips
2 eggs	oil for frying
4 oz. Mozzarella or Bel Paese cheese	1 further egg breadcrumbs

Mix together the rice and beaten eggs, and form into balls. Flatten each ball on the palm of your hand, and on the flattened surface lay a strip of ham and a strip of cheese. Close the ball together again, so that the rice conceals the contents. Continue till all the rice is used.

Finally dip the balls (*Suppli*, if you want the Italian name) in egg and breadcrumbs, and fry them in hot olive oil until they are a golden brown. Drain before serving.

SARTÙ

Rice does not appear on the Neapolitan menu nearly as frequently as do the various types of pasta, but there is one rice dish that is a speciality of Naples, and that, in spite of the length of time required for its preparation, is well worth trying, particularly at a time when you have available some turkey or chicken giblets — why not serve such a dish on Boxing Day, as a change from the cold left-overs from the Christmas turkey? The list of ingredients, though formidable, is not necessarily difficult to cope with. For 6 people you will need the following:

12 oz. rice
8 oz. lean beef passed
   through the mincer
1 egg plus 1 egg yolk
1 clove garlic, crushed
pepper and salt
chopped parsley
2 1-inch slices of bread
   with the crusts re-
   moved
flour
oil or lard for frying
about 8 oz. cooked
   green peas
4 oz. Bel Paese cheese
a little milk

4 oz. fresh mushrooms
   cut in small pieces or
   ½ oz. dried mush-
   rooms, reconstituted
   by soaking them in
   warm water for a few
   minutes
turkey or chicken
   giblets, a small
   chopped onion, a little
   chopped carrot
8 oz. Italian sausage
meat sauce (see page 230)
about 5 tablespoons
   grated Parmesan
crisp breadcrumbs

First of all, combine your minced lean beef, the bread — soaked in a little milk and squeezed dry — the garlic and chopped parsley with the beaten egg and egg yolk, together with the seasonings. Form into small balls or rissoles, and fry in hot oil until they are brown on both sides. Meanwhile, boil your rice in the approved fashion, in boiling, salted water and drain well. Cook the giblets with the exception of the liver, in a little water, with the chopped carrot and onion, for at least 2 hours, adding a bay leaf if the flavour is liked. 10 or 15 minutes before the end of this time, add the the liver and the sliced mushrooms. You are now ready to start composing your sartù. Butter a fireproof soufflé dish that is large enough to hold the combined ingredients, and after buttering it, sprinkle crisp breadcrumbs over the bottom and sides. Arrange about ¾ of the boiled rice in a layer covering the bottom and the sides of the soufflé dish, and in this casing place the meat balls, the giblets cut into pieces, the mushrooms, peas and the sausages cut in pieces. Over this pour the gravy from the giblets and sufficient meat sauce to moisten. Cut the cheese in small pieces and arrange on top, and finally cover with the balance of the boiled rice, and pour over a little more of the meat and tomato sauce, so that the dish is moist but not 'mushy'. Sprinkle with a fairly heavy layer of crisp breadcrumbs and the grated Parmesan cheese. Bake in a moderate oven for 30 minutes. The ingredients suggested are, so to speak, the bare minimum, you may add to the glory and mystery of your sartù by varying the ingredients with a little chopped ham or breast of turkey or chicken cut small, and if you wish to be particularly luxurious, hard-boil a couple of eggs, cut them in 4 lengthways and arrange them on the top of the dish before adding the final layer of rice.

FRIED RICE

TO SERVE 4

4 oz. left-over boiled rice	4 rashers streaky bacon
4 scrambled eggs	1 chopped onion
	salt and pepper to taste

Cut bacon into 1-inch pieces, and fry; chop onion, add to bacon and fry until it is golden; stir in the rice and fry till light brown, and at last minute stir in the scrambled eggs, season and mix well.

RICE SOUFFLÉ WITH CHICKEN LIVERS

TO SERVE 6

8 oz. rice	2 pints chicken stock
4 oz. butter	3 tablespoons Marsala
8 oz. chicken livers	2 tablespoons grated
4 eggs	Parmesan

Cook the rice for 20 minutes in the chicken stock, and at the end of that time stir in the cheese, butter and the chicken livers which have been cut in strips, floured lightly and fried in a little butter and the Marsala. Allow the mixture to cool, and then stir in the beaten yolks of the eggs and mix well. Beat the egg whites stiff, and fold into the mixture. Grease a soufflé dish that is large enough to hold the whole mixture, line it with buttered paper, and pour in your soufflé mixture, and cook in a moderate oven for about 15 minutes.

RICE SOUFFLÉ WITH SHRIMPS

TO SERVE 6

Proceed as for the foregoing recipe, but substituting for the chicken broth either water in which fish has been boiled, or failing that, plain water; and for the chicken livers, 8 oz. of shelled shrimps or prawns.

Polenta

One more of the farinaceous foods beloved by Italians is the yellow maize flour, known as polenta, which can be obtained in Italian provision shops and delicatessens. It can be bought either finely or coarsely ground, depending on the taste of the consumer.

It appears frequently on the tables of the north of Italy, frequently being used in lieu of bread, and although the plain boiled polenta is stodgy and uninteresting, if it is allowed to cool, it can be cut into slices, or formed into small dumplings, something after the style of gnocchi, and can form the basis of a good many agreeable dishes.

To cook sufficient polenta for four people, start off with six to eight ounces of the finely ground variety. Bring a pint of water to the boil in a fairly large saucepan, and to this add the polenta and cook slowly for about twenty minutes, stirring all the time. At the end of this time it should be thick and smooth.

Spread it on a large plate that has been rinsed with cold water, allow to cool, and then either cut it into slices, or with floured hands form it into little dumplings the size of a small egg.

The following are one or two ways in which the cooked product may be used.

BATUFFOLI AL SUGO
TO SERVE 4

Prepare 8 oz. finely ground polenta as directed on previous pages, and when cool form into little dumplings. Butter a fireproof dish, and in it lay a layer of these dumplings. When the first layer is completed, cover with a meat sauce and sprinkle generously with grated Parmesan, and on top place a second layer, continuing the layers until the dumplings are all used. Sprinkle little dabs of butter on the top layer, and a generous sprinkling of grated Parmesan; place in a hot oven for a few moments to allow the cheese to melt and serve very hot.

POLENTA AND CHEESE
TO SERVE 4

Cook 8 oz. polenta as previously directed, spreading on a moistened dish or a marble slab to cool. Cut into slabs and lay these in a buttered fireproof dish, sprinkling generous helpings of grated Parmesan between the layers, and seasoning with salt and a little cayenne. Cover top layer with grated cheese and a little butter, and bake in a hot oven until brown. Serve very hot.

POLENTA WITH TOMATO SAUCE
TO SERVE 4

½ pint hot water
½ pint milk
8 oz. finely ground
  polenta
pepper and salt to taste

8 tablespoons grated
  Parmesan
oil for frying
1 egg
fine breadcrumbs

Cook the polenta for 30 minutes in a double boiler in the hot water and milk which have been mixed and brought to the boil. At the last minute stir in cheese and seasonings, and stir until thoroughly mixed. Spread on a moistened dish to cool.

Beat the egg and when the polenta is cold, cut into slices, dip in egg and breadcrumbs and fry in hot olive oil until brown. Serve hot with tomato sauce (see page 217).

If you don't object to the slight stodginess, you may eat your polenta as it comes out of the saucepan, hot, without first waiting for it to cool, with any of the meat or tomato sauces under the heading of *Sauces*, or just with butter and cheese, but for the average English palate, the cooled and fried or baked variety is preferable.

There is a delicious sausage dish made with polenta that rather puts the English 'Sausage Toad' in the shade. For it you need 8 oz. polenta cooked as directed in boiling, salted water; unsweetened tomato sauce (see page 218), and 1 lb. Italian sausages, or failing these, chipolata. Cut the sausages into 1-inch lengths, and fry until they are brown, then pour over them the tomato sauce and mix well together. When the polenta is cooked, spread one half of it in a buttered fireproof dish, and over this pour one half of the sauce; add a second layer of polenta and the balance of the sauce. Sprinkle with grated Parmesan and place in a hot oven for a few moments so that the cheese melts and browns a trifle. Serve very hot.

CECI

Chick peas

These small, hard, yellow dried peas *must* be soaked overnight, and need long slow cooking in salted water to which ½ teaspoon bicarbonate of soda has been added to each quart of water. Cook until tender. When cold they go well with salad, seasoned with oil and vinegar or lemon juice.

CECI ALLA MARINARA

Chick peas, sailors' style
TO SERVE 4

1 lb. chick peas, prepared as suggested above pepper	2 or 3 tablespoons oil 4 anchovies 1 tablespoon chopped parsley

Having cooked the soaked peas till tender, allow them to keep hot in the water in which they have been cooked. Meanwhile, heat the oil, and to it add the anchovies cut small, the parsley and pepper to taste; mix well. Drain the *ceci*, and over them pour the prepared sauce, mixing well before serving.

Omelettes,
Egg and Cheese Dishes

If you are a lover of the light, fluffy omelette produced by the deft hands of the English or French omelette maker, you had better not order an omelette in Italy, for it is a heavier affair, it will be cooked in oil, and its filling, if it is a filled omelette, will be over-generous. If, however, you like your omelettes solid and substantial, you will be on safe ground.

Here is a typical Italian recipe for an omelette, which can be made *asciutta* or *morbida*, that is to say, dry, or not so dry, and of the two, the latter more nearly resembles the omelette of France or England.

FRITTATA SEMPLICE
Plain Omelette

TO SERVE 3

6 eggs	2 tablespoons olive oil
pinch salt	

Break eggs into a basin, and beat them until well mixed but not frothy, adding salt. Meanwhile in a heavy frying pan, preferably one kept only for the making of omelettes, heat olive oil and cook over moderate heat, lifting the edges from time to time with a spatula so that the uncooked portion can reach the bottom of the pan and become cooked. Continue until there is no liquid remaining. Then, if you are an expert pancake tosser, and only then, toss the omelette so as to reverse it. If you are not so skilled, turn it with a metal slice and allow the other side to cook. Turn on to a heated dish and serve very hot.

So much for the *Frittata Asciutta*, the dry omelette. If you prefer the more digestible *Frittata Morbida* cook the omelette on the one side, lifting the edges so that the liquid portion may reach the bottom of the pan and become cooked; form it with the spatula into an oval shape, and without turning, slip it on to a heated oval dish and serve immediately.

OMELETTE WITH HERBS

Using the same basic recipe and procedure, try your omelette with the addition of a little chopped parsley, a little chopped basil or thyme, or a combination of several chopped herbs, and as an experiment, try the addition of a very little chopped rosemary.

FRITTATA AI TARTUFI
Truffle omelette

Again starting with the basic omelette recipe, before turning it into the frying pan, add a finely chopped black or white truffle.

FRITTATA AI FUNGHI

Omelette with mushrooms

While you are preparing the eggs, sauté 4 oz. mushrooms cut in small pieces in a little butter and add to the omelette as it is beginning to cook, with a spatula fold the cooked portion over the mushrooms so that by the time the dish is completely cooked the filling is enveloped in the egg mixture, slide on to a heated oval platter and serve very hot.

FRITTATA ALLA SALSA DI POMODORO

Omelette with tomato sauce

Before cooking, add 2 tablespoons tomato sauce (see page 217) to the egg mixture.

FRITTATA AL FORMAGGIO

Cheese Omelette

To the basic egg mixture add 1 oz. grated Parmesan cheese before starting the cooking process.

FRITTATA AI LEGUMI

Vegetable Omelette

If you have 4 oz. cooked young green peas, or a similar amount of cooked asparagus tips, add these to the omelette as it is beginning to cook and proceed as suggested for *Frittata al Funghi*.

FRITTATA AL PROSCIUTTO
Ham Omelette

Cut 2 or 3 thin slices of ham into small pieces, and add to the eggs before starting to cook; proceed as suggested for *Frittata Semplice*. If liked, a little Italian salami may be substituted for the ham.

FRITTATA ALLA CIPOLLA
Onion Omelette

Chop a medium sized onion into small pieces and brown in a little butter; when cooked add to the basic egg mixture before starting to cook the omelette.

FRITTATA FARCITA
Stuffed omelette

Heat a little butter in a separate frying pan and in it combine 12 oz. mushrooms cut in small pieces, 1 tablespoon finely chopped fresh parsley, salt and pepper to taste and 1 tablespoon of cream. Allow to cook together for 5 minutes. Meanwhile make an omelette as suggested for *Frittata Semplice*, and when the underside is lightly cooked, pour on the sauce, and continue cooking, wrapping the egg mixture gradually around the filling. Serve very hot.

FRITTATA DI PATATE
Potato omelette
TO SERVE 4

Boil 4 medium sized potatoes in salted water, and when cooked, drain and mash well, or pass through a ricer. Mix with the lightly beaten yolks of 4 eggs, and a tablespoon of chopped parsley, and, if liked, a pinch of cinnamon; finally stir in the stiffly beaten whites of the eggs, and fry, first on one side and then on the other, in hot butter. Serve hot.

FRITTATA AI CARCIOFI
Artichoke omelette

For this the small globe artichokes which can be purchased preserved are used. The fresh vegetables are, of course, preferable, but are not always easy to obtain in this country. Take half a dozen of the artichokes, drain well, cut in pieces and fry lightly in a little butter, meanwhile preparing your *Frittata Semplice*, and adding the artichokes as suggested for the sauce in *Frittata Farcita*, just as the underside of the omelette is cooked, and wrapping the egg gradually around the artichokes so that by the time the omelette finishes cooking they are encased in it.

Now for a really 'solid' omelette.

FRITTATA COL RISO
Rice omelette
TO SERVE 4

1 pint milk	3 oz. rice
4 eggs	2 oz. grated Parmesan
1 oz. butter	a pinch of cinnamon
salt to taste	

Heat the milk and rice in a double boiler and allow to cook gently until the rice is tender and the milk absorbed (about 1 hour or a little longer). Stir in the butter, grated cheese, cinnamon and salt, and when it has cooled somewhat, add the eggs, beaten lightly. Mix well, and fry in hot butter, first on one side and then on the other, or if preferred, bake in a buttered soufflé dish in a moderate oven till browned.

Solid, but satisfying, this one.

UOVA STRACCIATI AL FORMAGGIO

Scrambled eggs with cheese
TO SERVE 4

6 eggs	2 oz. butter
1½ to 2 oz. grated	a little cream if
Parmesan	available

Beat the eggs lightly, adding a tablespoon of cream if available. Meanwhile warm the butter in a small stewpan, pour in the egg mixture, and cook over moderate heat, stirring continually, until the eggs are scrambled; at the last moment stir in the grated cheese and serve immediately on buttered toast.

UOVA COL RISO

Eggs with rice
TO SERVE 4

If you have about 4 oz. cold boiled rice, this is a good way of using it up.

Allow 2 eggs per person, place them in boiling water and allow them to cook for not longer than 5 minutes, and as soon as they are sufficiently cool to handle, shell them. Meanwhile, prepare 8 small ramekin dishes by greasing fairly liberally with butter, and placing a little rice in the bottom of each; place a shelled egg on top of the rice, and cover with a teaspoon of grated Parmesan and dot with butter. They can then be 'poached', by placing the dishes in a shallow pan with hot water half way up the sides of the dishes, and cooking over moderate heat for about 5 minutes or until the cheese melts, or alternatively they may be baked in the oven for a similar length of time.

FRIED CHEESE

For each person allow 2 slices of Bel Paese about the size of half a slice of bread and cut very thin. Flour lightly, and dip first in beaten egg and then in breadcrumbs and fry golden brown, first on one side then on the other in hot butter, Drain to remove surplus fat. Serve very hot.

Fish

Have you ever stopped to consider the lack of imagination shown by the average — and I mean the average, not the exceptional — housewife where the cooking and serving of fish are concerned? Yet look at the variety of fish obtainable at most fishmongers' shops, and you'll probably agree that there's no real reason for our slavish adherence to boiled cod, fish and chips, soused herrings — delicious though they undoubtedly are, with crab or lobster, or a few shrimps or prawns for a special treat. There's really no reason on earth why Friday, Fish Day, should not produce the tastiest and most exciting meals of the week. Take a look and see what our friends, the Italians, do about fish. To be sure, fish such as octopus and squid are not easily come by over here, and many of us wouldn't fancy eating them if they were, and for scampi we may have to make do with Dublin Bay prawns, but remembering the galaxy of fish now at our disposal, we can enlarge our repertoire of dishes very considerably. The following few recipes are offered in the hope that they will encourage experiments.

FISH FRIED IN THE SICILIAN WAY

Try this now and again as an alternative to our own more conservative methods of cooking.

First prepare your fish by cleaning, washing and wiping dry, and finally dipping in flour.

Then in a heavy pan heat a good layer of good quality olive oil; when it is really hot, sprinkle generously with salt and when it is smoking put in your prepared fish, brown quickly on both sides, cover the pan, and lower the heat until the fish is cooked through. Serve very hot.

FISH AU GRATIN
Pesce gratinato
TO SERVE 6

6 oz. rice	8 oz. butter
1 lb. floury potatoes	12 oz. previously boiled
2 tablespoons flour	fish, from which skin
¼ pint milk	and bones have been
2 tablespoons grated	removed
Parmesan	breadcrumbs

Cook the rice as directed on page 95; when cooked and drained, replace in saucepan, mix with beaten egg yolk and 6 oz. of butter, and allow to keep warm until the butter is absorbed. Meanwhile cook and mash the potatoes with a little butter.

Prepare a béchamel sauce of 2 oz. butter, 2 tablespoons flour and ¼ pint or slightly more of hot milk.

Flake the fish finely.

Having made these preparations, butter a fireproof dish and in it place the rice, forming a flat 'bed' on which to place the flaked fish. Form a border with the mashed potato; pour the béchamel over the fish, and add a layer of Parmesan, grated and mixed with crisp breadcrumbs. Cook in a hot oven until the Parmesan has melted and the béchamel has taken on a golden colour.

FISH CAKES

TO SERVE 4

about 8 oz. each of cold fish, and mashed potatoes	1 tablespoon chopped parsley 1 egg beaten pepper and salt

Flake the fish and combine with the potatoes, seasonings and egg; form into small cakes and fry until brown on both sides in hot butter or hot olive oil.

COD AU GRATIN

Allow 1 middle cod steak per person and allow to marinate by laying it in a flat dish and covering with 2 tablespoons oil, the juice of 1 lemon and pepper and salt to taste. After 2 hours drain, sprinkle with breadcrumbs and grill on a hot grill first on one side then on the other.

GRILLED SOLE

As with cod, allow your sole to marinate for 2 hours in a marinade composed of 2 tablespoons oil, the juice of a ½ lemon — or a whole lemon if liked — pepper and salt to taste; drain, cover with breadcrumbs and grill on a hot grill.

In Tuscany there is a favourite fish dish, very rich, and rather indigestible, but, having been warned, you may still wish to try it:

CACCIUCCO ALLA TOSCANA

This dish is interesting if an assortment of fish is used. Try the combination of sole with red mullet. Wash and clean your fish and wipe dry.

Meanwhile, in a stewpan heat a couple of tablespoons of olive oil and in it brown a chopped onion, a crushed clove of garlic and a little chopped parsley; add rather more than 8 oz. fresh tomatoes, peeled and cut in small pieces, pepper and salt; when the tomatoes are cooked, add the juice of ½ lemon, boil for a few minutes longer and then pass through a sieve or a food mill. Return the strained sauce to the stewpan, and in it cook your fish for 30 minutes or until tender; finally add a further tablespoon of oil. Serve the fish on a heated dish with the sauce poured over and with it serve fingers of toast with which to soak up the sauce — you have been warned, this dish is rich, and somewhat indigestible.

ARAGOSTA LESSATA
Boiled lobster

You'll probably prefer to buy him ready boiled, but if you can bear to cope with the live beast, he's much better boiled at home. Place your lobster in a deep saucepan of boiling water, so that he is completely covered, and boil him for 45 minutes if he is a large fellow, 30 minutes for his smaller brother, and at the end of that time, if you are going to eat him hot, remove him from the water, rub the shell with a little olive oil to brighten the colour, and split him in two lengthways. Serve with olive oil, lemon and salt and pepper.

COLD LOBSTER

Allow your lobster to cool before cutting open lengthways, then crack the claws so that the meat may be extracted easily, and serve with a green salad dressed with oil and lemon juice.

FRIED LOBSTER

Having prepared your lobster, remove the meat from the body and the claws, dip them first in oil and then in flour seasoned with pepper and salt, or in a frying batter and fry in hot oil. Serve with sections of lemon.

CRAWFISH

These, known in some districts as 'lobster tails', may be substituted for lobster in any of the foregoing recipes.

SOFT SHELL CRABS

These are tiny crabs caught at a time when they are changing their shells, and they are considered a delicacy in early May in Venice. Minus their shells the crabs rise to the surface of the water and are caught in great quantities. The method is to flour them and fry them while still alive in boiling oil — delicious if you like them and can forget the wholesale murder that has taken place to provide you with your dainty dish.

CALAMARETTI

Again a dish met with along the Adriatic coast, where baby inkfish the size of large house spiders are fried whole in butter, often accompanied by scampi — truly worth trying and rather less off-putting than the soft shell crabs if you are of a squeamish nature.

If you are a lover of eels, here are a few typically Italian ways of preparing them.

ANGUILLA ALLA FERRARESE

Eels as served in Ferrara

TO SERVE 4

1½ lb. eels, cleaned and cut in 1-inch slices	salt and pepper
3 tablespoons white wine	a pinch of mixed spice
1 bay leaf	a pinch of thyme
a little butter	1 egg lightly beaten
	breadcrumbs

Having prepared the eels, place in a casserole and over them pour the wine mixed with the spices and herbs, add the bay leaf. Cover and cook in a moderate oven for 45 minutes. At the end of that time, lift the eels from the sauce, drain, dip in oiled butter, then in beaten egg and breadcrumbs flavoured if liked with a little nutmeg, and fry brown on both sides in hot butter.

ROAST EELS

Large eels may be cut in thickish slices and cooked on a spit, with a bay leaf or two and a sprig of rosemary interspersed for flavour, and basted from time to time with olive oil and sprinkled with salt. Since we cannot always cook in this fashion, the next best thing is to lay the slices in a flat dish, and pour over them 2 tablespoons olive oil seasoned with salt and pepper and the juice of a ½ lemon; allow them to remain in this marinade for at least an ½ hour, turning them from time to time so that it may penetrate the fish, then place in an oiled fireproof dish, and bake in a hot oven till tender, basting from time to time with the marinade.

ROAST EELS
A variation

Instead of a bay leaf or two, use the same number of bruised leaves of sage, and so that the flavour may penetrate, lay the fish, when it comes to roasting it, on the sage leaves in an oiled fireproof dish.

STEWED EELS
TO SERVE 4

1½ lb. eels
1 tablespoon oil
2 leaves sage, chopped
1 clove garlic
1 oz. butter
1 teaspoon chopped parsley
1 gill white wine

Skin and clean the eels and cut in pieces about 2 inches in length. Melt the oil and butter together in a stewpan, add the herbs, the garlic and the eels, and the wine; cover closely and cook over moderate heat for 45 minutes, adding a little water from time to time if it shows signs of drying up.

ARINGA ALLA GRATELLA
Grilled herrings
TO SERVE 4

8 medium sized herrings
a little milk

Clean the herrings and split them open, removing the backbone. Lay them in a flat dish and cover with a little milk and leave them to soak for a couple of hours. Drain; oil them lightly, and grill on a hot grill, serving them with sections of lemon.

MERLUZZO ALLA FIORENTINA

Cod as cooked in Florence

TO SERVE 4

6 cod steaks
salt and pepper
1 gill white wine

a little chopped fennel
oil
flour

Oil a flat fireproof dish and in it place the lightly floured
steaks of cod and over them pour a tablespoon of olive oil,
the fennel, pepper and salt and white wine and bake in
a moderate oven for 30 minutes, basting at intervals with the
sauce.

MERLUZZO IN SALSA

Cod with tomatoes

TO SERVE 4

6 cod steaks
1 tablespoon olive oil

6 tomatoes, skinned and
   cut in pieces
1 small onion chopped

Heat the oil in a stewpan and in it brown the onion; add
the tomato cut small and cook together for 5 minutes, add
the fish, cover the pan and cook over moderate heat 30 minutes.

SALT COD

We are apt to turn up our noses at the grey slabs of salt
cod we see hanging in a fishmonger's shop, but the Italian
cook can teach us several good ways of serving this ill-
favoured fish.

First of all it must be remembered that in order to render
it acceptable at all it should be soaked for at least 24 hours,
and if this can be done in running water, so much the better;
failing that, change the water several times during the soaking
process. At the end of the time, skin the fish, and remove the
bones before starting any cooking experiments with it. In
Italy it goes under two names, baccala and stoccafisso.

STOCCAFISSO IN SALSA

Salt cod in sauce

TO SERVE 4

2 lb. salt cod, soaked for at least 24 hours, skinned and boned

2 tablespoons olive oil

1 medium sized beetroot

salt and pepper

1 medium onion chopped small

1 celery stalk chopped

2 tablespoons tomato sauce (see page 217)

Heat the oil in a stewpan and in it brown the onion for a few minutes, then add the beetroot, washed and cut in cubes, the celery, the cod, cut in small pieces, the salt and pepper and cook very slowly for at least 2 hours; when the beetroot is tender, add the tomato sauce and from time to time add a little water if the dish shows signs of drying.

A variation

Using the preceding recipe, substitute for the tomato sauce 2 tablespoons white wine.

STOCCAFISSO ALLA LIGURE

Salt cod as cooked in Liguria

TO SERVE 4

2 lb. salt cod, soaked in water for at least 24 hours, skinned, boned and cut in small pieces

1 onion cut in small pieces	4 tomatoes, skinned and seeded
1 small carrot cut in cubes	1 tablespoon olive oil
1 tablespoon chopped parsley	1 clove garlic, crushed
pepper, salt and nutmeg	1 stick celery cut small
	2 anchovies cut small
	4 oz. fresh mushrooms
	1 tablespoon flour

Heat the oil in a stewpan, and in it cook the chopped vegetables and anchovies for a few minutes, sprinkle with the flour, and add slowly about a ½ pint warm water, stirring constantly. Finally add the fish, cut small, cover the stewpan and cook slowly for 2 hours or a little longer, adding more water from time to time if the dish looks like becoming too dry.

CREAM OF BACCALA

Creamed salt cod

TO SERVE 4

2 lb. best cut of salt cod, soaked 24 hours, skinned and boned and then steamed for 1½ hours

Pound the fish in a mortar, adding a little olive oil from time to time and working till the whole is reduced to a creamy mass, adding, if it appears too dry, a little warm milk. At the end of the pounding, re-heat in a double boiler, then pile on a warmed dish and serve with slices of crisply fried bread.

POLPETTINE DI STOCCAFISSO
Rissoles of salt cod
TO SERVE 4

2 lb. salt cod, prepared
as for cream of bac-
cala and allowed to
cool

2 beaten eggs
1 tablespoon chopped
parsley
a pinch of thyme

Mix well together and form into small flat rissoles. Fry in
hot oil and serve with sections of lemon.

TUNNY AS COOKED IN LIGURIA
TO SERVE 4

1 lb. tunny *ventresca*
cut in thin slices
2 anchovies
½ oz. dried mushrooms,
reconstituted by
soaking in warm wa-
ter for 10 minutes
pepper and salt

1 clove garlic, crushed
1 heaped tablespoon
chopped fresh parsley
2 tablespoons olive oil
½ pint white wine
1 tablespoon flour
½ lemon
butter

Heat the oil, add the flour, then slowly add the wine, the
anchovies pounded to a paste and the other ingredients,
except for the fish; allow to cook together for 10 minutes,
stirring frequently. Add the tunny fish, and pepper and salt
to taste; cover the stewpan, and lower the heat, allowing
to cook slowly for 45 minutes. Remove the fish to a hot dish,
and to the sauce add a piece of butter the size of a walnut,
and the juice of ½ lemon; bring this to boiling point and
pour over the fish and serve hot.

TUNNY FISH AS COOKED IN SICILY

For this dish the fresh tunny is needed, and the best cut is the stomach *(ventresca)*, of which you should allow one thin slice per person.

Lay the slices in a flat dish and cover with a dressing composed of 1½ tablespoons white wine, salt, pepper, a pinch of nutmeg and the juice of ½ lemon, and allow them to remain in this dressing for 2 hours, turning them from time to time so that the dressing can penetrate well. Drain, sprinkle with a little chopped fresh rosemary and a little crushed garlic, and grill on both sides on a hot grill, basting it with the dressing. When it is nicely browned on both sides, decorate it with one or two anchovies cut in strips before sending it to the table.

TUNNY WITH PEAS

Again for this dish you need thin slices of fresh tunny, remembering that the *ventresca* is the best cut. Brown on both sides in hot oil in a heavy pan, then add a medium sized onion chopped finely, and a teaspoon of finely chopped fresh parsley, and cook all together for 10 minutes. Meanwhile, partly cook some fresh green peas, allowing 3 or 4 oz. when shelled to each slice of tunny fish; drain and add to the pan in which the fish is cooking, add 2 tablespoons boiling water, and a similar quantity of tomato sauce (see page 217) for each slice of fish, cover and cook slowly for a further 20 minutes.

TRIGLIE ALLA TRIESTINA

Red mullet as cooked in Trieste

TO SERVE 4

4 red mullet of medium
  size
juice of ½ lemon
3 tablespoons white wine

1 tablespoon olive oil
1 tablespoon chopped
  capers

Heat together in a heavy pan the oil, lemon juice, capers and
wine, and after 10 minutes add the cleaned fish and allow
to cook for 20 minutes, turning the fish carefully at the end
of half this time. Serve hot.

TRIGLIE ALLA LIVORNESE

Red mullet Leghorn style

Allow one medium-sized red mullet per person. Remove the
inside, the fins and the scales and wash well. Lay the fish
side by side in a flat dish in which you have prepared a
soffritto of 1 tablespoon olive oil, a clove of garlic crushed,
a little chopped fennel, salt and pepper, and cook in a hot
oven for 10 minutes; then cover with tomato sauce (see
page 217), lower the heat slightly and allow to finish cooking
for a further 30 minutes in a moderate oven.

FRIED RED MULLET

1 medium sized fish
  per person
2 tablespoons olive oil
1 tablespoon capers

salted anchovies
1 clove garlic, crushed
1 tablespoon chopped
  parsley

Heat the oil, and in it fry the chopped anchovies, and allow the mullet to brown first on one side and then on the other; when brown, sprinkle over the fish the parsley and crushed garlic, lower the heat and allow to finish cooking — the mullet need about 15 minutes cooking in all; just before removing from the fire, add capers to the sauce and pour over the fish when serving.

TRIGLIE ALLA LIGURE

Red mullet as cooked in Liguria

TO SERVE 4

4 medium sized red
  mullet
1 tablespoon chopped
  parsley
2 anchovies cut in
  small pieces
1 tablespoon olive oil
½ pint tomato sauce

1 chopped onion
a little chopped
  fennel
½ oz. dried mushrooms
  reconstituted in warm
  water
3 tablespoons white
  wine

Heat the oil in a heavy pan and in it place the onion, parsley, fennel and chopped mushrooms and anchovies, and allow to cook together for 5 minutes, then add the tomato sauce and white wine and cook for a further 20 minutes, stirring frequently. Meanwhile clean and prepare the fish and lay them side by side in a flat earthenware dish. When the sauce is cooked, pour over the fish, and place in a hot oven and cook for 20 minutes.

A GENOESE WAY OF COOKING FISH

This method may be used to advantage when cooking trout, cod fillets, carp, eels, mackerel, etc. After preparing the fish for cooking, lay it in a stewpan, and cover with the following sauce, allowing it to cook gently for 20 or 30 minutes or until tender.

SAUCE

1 tablespoon olive oil
1 chopped onion
1½ tablespoons white wine
½ oz. dried mushrooms
salt and pepper
2 oz. butter

1 tablespoon flour
½ pint water or fish stock
1 tablespoon tomato sauce (see page 217)
1 or 2 anchovies cut small

Heat the oil and in it brown the onion. Then add the butter, and stir in the flour; slowly add the wine, water and tomato sauce, stirring all the time to make sure the mixture does not stick to the bottom of the pan; add the dried mushrooms, reconstituted in a little warm water and cut small, and the anchovies and seasonings. Cook together for 10 minutes, then pass through a sieve, and use as suggested above. Just before serving, remove the fish and keep hot, and add to the sauce the juice of ½ lemon; cook the sauce for a further 2 or 3 minutes and when serving, pour over the cooked fish.

SCAMPI

The fish section of an Italian cookery book would be far from complete if no reference were made to 'scampi', those natives of the waters of the Adriatic that, though they resemble Dublin Bay prawns, are plumper and have a somewhat finer flavour. Since it is not easy to obtain 'scampi' at one's local fishmongers, Dublin Bay prawns may be substituted, though with a wistful thought for the finer flavour the dish would have 'if only' one were on the shores of the Adriatic and able to obtain the right ingredient with ease.

SCAMPI ALLA LOMBARDA
Scampi as cooked in Lombardy
TO SERVE 4

36 to 40 scampi or
   Dublin Bay prawns
3 tablespoons white
   wine vinegar
1 bay leaf
1 clove garlic crushed

4 cloves
½ small onion, chopped
   small
1 tablespoon chopped
   parsley
a little chopped fennel
salt to taste

Mix together all the ingredients except the fish, and cook together for 5 minutes in a stewpan; then add the fish, removed from shell, cover, and cook over a medium heat for 15 or 20 minutes, stirring from time to time. Serve very hot.

If liked, shrimps may be substituted for the scampi in the foregoing recipe.

SCAMPI ALLA MODENESE
Scampi as cooked in Modena
TO SERVE 4

36 to 40 scampi or
   Dublin Bay Prawns
1 oz. butter
1 tablespoon chopped
   parsley
a little chopped thyme

1 small onion chopped
   fine
1 small carrot, diced
3 tablespoons white
   wine
3 tablespoons white
   vinegar

Heat the butter, add the other ingredients, with the exception of the fish and cook together for 15 minutes. Meanwhile prepare the fish, add them to the sauce and cook over a moderate flame for a further 15 minutes. Serve hot, covered with the sauce.

FRIED SCAMPI

For this you may suit your own particular fancy; allowing 10 or a dozen per person, remove the shells, and fry the fish in any of these three ways:

Dust lightly with flour and fry in hot olive oil, serving with sections of lemon.

Dip first in beaten egg and then in crisp breadcrumbs and fry in hot oil or hot butter and serve with sections of lemon.

Dip in a light frying batter and fry in hot butter, again serving with sections of lemon.

STURGEON, HOUSEWIFE STYLE

TO SERVE 4

1 lb. sturgeon cut into thin slices	2 slices bread, soaked in milk and squeezed dry
1 chopped onion	
1 tablespoon chopped fresh parsley	3 tablespoons sherry
salt and pepper	1 egg, beaten lightly
a pinch of nutmeg	breadcrumbs for coating

Mix together the chopped onion, parsley, salt, pepper, nutmeg and soaked bread, and use as a filling between each two slices of the fish. Dip the 'sandwiches' in the beaten egg and then in breadcrumbs, and fry in hot butter, first on one side and then on the other, then pour over them the sherry, and allow to cook all together for 15 minutes. Serve hot with the sauce poured over the slices of fish.

NASELLO CON PISELLI

Whiting with peas

TO SERVE 4

4 whiting
1 tablespoon chopped parsley
1 lb. shelled green peas
salt

1 medium sized onion, chopped fine
1 tablespoon oil
1 tablespoon tomato conserve

Half cook the peas in boiling salted water and drain. Meanwhile, heat the oil in a stewpan, and in it brown the onion, parsley and the whiting; when the whiting is browned on both sides, add the drained peas, and the tomato conserve diluted with a little boiling water, and allow to cook for a further 15 minutes over moderate heat.

CURLED WHITING

If you can persuade your fishmonger to prepare whiting in the old-fashioned way, skinning them and passing the tail through the eye sockets, allowing one per person, flour the fish lightly and fry a golden brown on both sides in hot butter in a heavy frying pan. Serve with sections of lemon.

TO POACH FISH

A wise precaution is to wrap fish intended for poaching in a piece of muslin; this prevents it breaking when it is removed from the saucepan in which it has poached.

Allow 10 minutes per lb.

Start your fish in cold water, in which you have placed 3 or 4 peppercorns, a bay leaf and either a tablespoon of vinegar or the juice of a ½ lemon, and bring it to the boil quite slowly; then allow it to simmer for the required time.

TO ROAST FISH

In a great many native Italian recipes you will notice the instruction to toast the fish *allo spiedo* (on a spit), and since this is an implement not often to be found in the English kitchen, roasting in the oven has to be substituted. The oven should be hot, and the fish scored across with a knife and brushed with olive oil, and placed on an oiled grid in a baking dish or tin. Allow about 10 minutes per lb. and baste from time to time with oil and any juices that may have fallen into the roasting dish. Sprinkle with salt before serving.

PESCI ACCARTOCCIATI
Fish in paper cases

You will need pieces of greaseproof paper, one for each piece of fish to be cooked, and of a size large enough to envelop the fish entirely and wrap well over so that no juices escape. Oil the pieces of paper on one side, and oil whatever fish you are planning to cook, and lay it on the paper, after sprinkling it with salt and pepper, a little chopped onion, a scraping of garlic, chopped parsley or other herbs you may fancy, a ½ bay leaf if you like the flavour. Close the paper by folding the edges together carefully so that the juices cannot escape, and cook in a moderate oven. The fish is served in its paper envelopes, so that each person may be served with the fish and sauce together.

This is an excellent method of cooking trout, steaks of salmon, steaks of turbot, cod or halibut, or whole prepared mackerel.

OSTRICHE ALLA VENEZIANA

Oysters, Venetian style

At the risk of being accused of heresy for suggesting methods of cooking oysters, I would suggest trying this Venetian method.

Allow half a dozen oysters per person; open the fish, loosen them in their shells, and to each add a little of the following mixture:

MIXTURE

1 tablespoon chopped
  fresh parsley
1 stalk of celery chopped
  finely
1 clove garlic, crushed

a pinch of chopped
  fresh thyme
pepper to taste
1 tablespoon crisp
  breadcrumbs

Add a few drops of olive oil before grilling under a hot grill. Serve with sections of lemon.

PIGS IN BLANKETS

Oysters again, and oysters cooked. Allow 6 per person, remove from the shells, wrap each oyster in a strip of ham or streaky bacon, and fry in hot butter.

OR WITHOUT BLANKETS

Omitting the wrapping of ham or bacon, dip the shelled oysters first in beaten egg and then in breadcrumbs and fry in hot butter. Serve with sections of lemon.

FRITTO MISTO MARE
Mixed Fried Fish

If you go to Italy and having visited a town on the coast come away without having eaten at least one dish of *Fritto Misto Mare*, then you might almost as well have stayed at home. In Venice you will probably be served with a mixture of tiny octopus, not much larger than a hefty house spider, scampi, and minute mullet, all dipped in a light batter and fried in hot oil, drained and served with sections of lemon.

Farther south you may meet some peculiar white circles in your *Fritto Misto Mare* that have a more than slight resemblance in texture to the pencil eraser of school days. Rubber it isn't, but ink-fish it is, and it should previously have undergone a fairly lengthy operation of skinning, having its insides removed, its eyes and ink-bag removed also, and the balance boiled until tender, and this may take up to an hour if you want to avoid that too-great resemblance to pencil eraser texture. When tender, and not before, the ink-fish should be cut into rings, and if you're frying your own *Fritto Misto Mare*, allow 6 of these per person, with the same number of scampi and one or two tiny mullet.

CLAMS OR MUSSELS COOKED WITH EGGS

Allow about 1½ pints of the fish per person.

Before cooking, leave them in slightly salted water for 2 hours so that they may open and the sand may come out of them.

Meanwhile prepare in a heavy pan a *soffritto* of two tablespoons of oil in which you have browned a small chopped onion and 1 teaspoon of chopped parsley; add the fish and, when they are opened, add the beaten yolks of 2 or 3 eggs, depending on the quantity of fish, and the juice of a ½ lemon. Stir the mixture, and keep it just below boiling point, and serve as soon as it is well mixed.

CLAMS or MUSSELS, FISHERMEN'S STYLE

Having cleaned the fish, place them in a covered pan over a fairly strong heat until they begin to open; uncover the pan at this point, and sprinkle the fish with chopped parsley and crushed garlic, and serve as soon as all are opened. You will find they make sufficient juice of their own not to require additional liquid.

SOLE WITH WHITE WINE

Allow 1 medium sized sole per person. Skin and remove the head and fins and dust with flour. Heat a little butter in a heavy pan until it bubbles, lay in the fish and cook first on one side then the other, then pour over it 2 tablespoons white wine for each fish, and a little fish stock made from boiling together the head, skin and fins. Reduce the heat and cook gently until tender, by which time the sauce will have reduced in volume. When serving, strain the sauce over the fish.

It is well worth trying cider instead of white wine.

SOLE FRIED IN OIL

Allow 1 medium sized fish per person; skin, remove head and fins. Dip first in flour and then in beaten egg, and fry quickly, first on one side then on the other, in hot oil until light golden brown. Serve very hot with sections of lemon.

PIKE
to be eaten cold

Prepare a good sized pike by scraping off the scales, removing the inside, and cutting off the fins. Tie in a cloth and place in a large saucepan or fish kettle with 2 tablespoons white wine, 1 gill water, a bay leaf, a pinch of thyme, a chopped carrot, a stalk of celery cut small, 1 tablespoon chopped parsley, a clove of garlic, 2 cloves and salt to taste. Bring to the boil and cook slowly, allowing 10 to 12 minutes per lb. When cooked, allow to cool in its own broth, then strain and serve cold with a piquant sauce.

Or, if you like, to be eaten hot

When the fish is cooked, instead of allowing it to cool, lift from the fish kettle, remove the cloth in which it has been cooked, and serve immediately with any sauce you fancy, either a piquant sauce, or one of the tomato sauces (see *Sauces*, pages 217—34).

PIKE AU GRATIN

Clean a medium sized pike and allow to marinate in olive oil for 30 minutes or so. Sprinkle with salt and crisp breadcrumbs and grill on both sides until brown. Serve hot with sections of lemon.

TROUT or CARP

These when cleaned may be prepared in a similar manner and are excellent.

Many Italian cooks prepare fish and meats by cooking on a spit; since this is an implement rarely to be found in English kitchens, English cooks have to content themselves by using a grill where a 'spit' has been prescribed.

TENCH

Having cleaned your tench, allow to marinate for 30 minutes in olive oil to which has been added a little chopped fresh rosemary, pepper and salt. Drain and grill on both sides and serve very hot.

GRILLED GREY MULLET

Allow 1 medium sized grey mullet per person. Scrape off the scales with the back of a knife, clean and wipe dry. Oil all over and sprinkle with salt and pepper, and cook on a hot grill, first on one side then on the other.

GRILLED RED MULLET

These should be eaten very fresh. Allow 1 fish per person. Scrape off the scales, and clean, removing all the inside except the liver; wash well, wipe dry, oil all over, sprinkle with pepper and salt and grill first on one side and then on the other and serve hot.

CAPPON MAGRO

If you are expecting guests for a buffet supper, and know them to be lovers of fish, you could prepare few things more appetising than this famous fish salad, originating in Genoa, but likely to be found in any seaside town in Italy. But be warned, it takes a lot of time for shopping and preparation, and it is costly. The recipe given below should prove sufficient for a party of eight or nine.

First of all, look out your handsomest round or oval serving dish, for this is a 'dressed up' dish. Next, if you want to do the job properly, procure 8 oz. ships' biscuits, break them up, and soak them overnight in 1 tablespoon of olive oil mixed with an equal quantity of vinegar. If you don't like the sound of the ships' biscuits, dry half a dozen slices of bread in the oven, and when they are crisp, treat them as suggested for the ships' biscuits. Next, prepare a selection of vegetables in season, say 8 oz. or more of small new potatoes, and similar quantities of shelled fresh green peas, French beans, young carrots, cauliflower; cook them separately in boiling, salted water — don't overcook — drain and set on one side. Prepare a head of celery, 8 oz. button mushrooms, 2 oz. black olives, a similar quantity of green olives, and 4 hard-boiled eggs; a small jar of preserved artichoke hearts would add interest to the dish; one or two small cooked beetroot would be colourful — and this is a dish where colour matters. Cut the mushrooms in pieces and marinate with a little oil and vinegar, pepper and salt.

Where fish is concerned, prepare a boiled lobster, a $\frac{1}{2}$ pint of shrimps or prawns; half a dozen scallops; and 2 lb. of some good white fish, turbot, sole or halibut.

Poach the white fish and the scallops for 7 minutes, lift from the water, flake and season with oil, lemon juice, pepper and salt. Shell the shrimps, and remove the lobster from its shell, and season these also with oil, lemon juice and pepper and salt.

Next prepare the special sauce for Cappon Magro:

SAUCE:

1 teaspoon chopped
    parsley
6 anchovies
1 tablespoon chopped
    nuts
a pinch of oregano
¼ pint olive oil
1 tablespoon grated
    fennel root

1 clove garlic
2 tablespoons capers
2 or 3 gherkins
4 egg yolks (2 raw,
    2 hard-boiled)
2 tablespoons vinegar
6 green olives
1 thick slice of bread,
    soaked in vinegar and
    squeezed dry

Place the parsley and garlic in a mortar and pound to a paste, add capers, olives (having removed the stones), gherkins, fennel, hard-boiled egg yolks, bread, nuts and oregano; when all pounded to a paste, slowly add the oil, the vinegar and the raw egg yolks, stirring with a wooden spoon; the finished sauce should have the consistency of mayonnaise.

All ingredients now being ready, you may start your dish. First of all arrange a platform of the ships' biscuits or bread, and on it spread a little of the sauce; next arrange the various ingredients attractively in pyramid fashion on the platform of ships' biscuits, a layer of flaked fish, a layer of assorted vegetables, a layer of the sauce and so on until all are used up. The bright-coloured vegetables, the sliced beetroot, peas and small or diced carrots, may be used as garnishes, as may a few unshelled prawns, the lobster claws, cracked for easy eating, and the quartered hard-boiled eggs. This dish should, of course, be served very cold, and the 'prettier' it is in appearance the better.

STURGEON

If you intend cooking a whole sturgeon, choose a fairly small fish. Scrape off the scales with the back of a knife, clean and remove the inside; wash and wipe dry. Make several small holes with the point of a knife and in these insert fillets of salted anchovy. Place in a vessel and cover with ½ pint oil, salt, and the juice of 2 lemons, a little chopped parsley and chopped thyme. Leave for 2 hours. Remove and drain; wrap in greaseproof paper and bake in a moderate oven for 1 hour; remove the paper and cook for a further 20 to 25 minutes, basting during this time with the mixture in which it was allowed to marinate. Serve very hot.

ROAST TUNNY FISH

After our own brief acquaintance with beige-coloured tunny fish in small tins, it is a startling thing to behold one's first piece of 'tunny in the raw', a huge, liver-coloured piece of fish on a fishmonger's slab in Naples or the towns of Sicily.

For roast tunny take a fairly thick slice of fresh tunny and place it in an earthenware vessel with 2 tablespoons oil, some chopped parsley, chopped onion, the juice of a lemon, one or two cloves and salt and pepper to taste. Allow it to remain in this marinade for a couple of hours, turning from time to time. Drain, sprinkle with breadcrumbs and bake in the oven for 1 hour or a little longer, basting from time to time with the marinating mixture.

SNAILS

You probably won't fancy them, and in any case you probably won't be obtaining the live snails in this country, but just in case you want to know, you have to starve the creatures for a fortnight so that they lose all their slime and scum. During this time, to prevent their wandering, you have to keep them in a basket, wrapping them loosely in a cloth, which for hygienic reasons it will pay you to change fairly frequently. If you can stand this test of endurance, at the end of the time soak the snails in salted water with a dash of vinegar for 3 or 4 hours, washing them after that in running water until there is no trace left of the scum or slime. Boil them next in salted water for 1½ hours, after which strain them and remove them from their shells, cutting away the black portion that you will find on the end of the body. After all this preparation, you may proceed to cook the snails as you fancy.

One good way is as follows:

50—60 prepared snails
1 tablespoon oil
1 clove garlic crushed
1 medium-sized onion
pinch chopped fresh
  rosemary
1 teaspoon chopped
  parsley
½ oz. dried mushrooms
  reconstituted in warm
  water and chopped
  small
2 tablespoons tomato
  sauce (see page 217)
1 gill white wine

Heat oil in a stewpan, and cook in it for 5 minutes garlic, onion, rosemary and parsley. Add shelled snails, chopped mushrooms and tomato sauce. Cook together for 10 minutes, then add white wine and allow to cook slowly for 10 minutes longer. Serve hot.

FROGS

The Italian variety make good eating. Try them fried. Skin
the frogs, removing the head and the inside, cutting off the
feet and washing them well, then leave to soak for 2 or 3 hours
in water to which a little salt has been added. Drain them
and then cut in pieces. Marinate for 1 hour in a little oil
to which you have added a chopped onion, a little parsley,
a bay leaf, a little chopped thyme and/or rosemary, pepper
and salt and the juice of a $\frac{1}{2}$ lemon. Drain, and flour them
lightly and fry in hot oil or butter.

Or for a more elaborate experiment try —

RANE ALLA GASTALDA

Prepare the frogs as suggested for fried frogs, but when they
have soaked in water 2 or 3 hours, dry them, but do not cut
them in pieces, truss them with the legs crossed over the
body, flour them lightly, then brown them in a stewpan with
a little butter flavoured with chopped parsley, a crushed
clove of garlic, pepper and salt. When they are browned
all over add a $\frac{1}{2}$ ounce of dried mushrooms reconstituted in
warm water and cut in pieces, and $\frac{1}{2}$ pint white wine, and
cook over moderate heat in a covered pan for 30 minutes
or until they are tender. Serve with sections of lemon.

Meats

The following pages give but a small selection from the numerous ways Italian cooks have of cooking beef, veal, mutton, pork, and the various edible entrails classed in English butchers' shops as 'offal'.

To the casual visitor to the country, it might appear that no calf is allowed to grow to maturity, since *vitello* (veal) makes so frequent an appearance on all menus, but living in the country one meets fairly frequently all the other meats, plus several unfamiliar to us, as, for example, young kid, which in taste greatly resembles lamb.

Sucking pig and equally youthful lambs are delicacies to be met with in Italy, and, despite their over-richness, they are delicious. Recipes for these have not been given, how-ever, since they are so rarely eaten outside Italy.

MANZO ALLA MASSAIA
Beef, domestic style

Cut 2 lb. stewing beef into small pieces and place in a stewpan with a little olive oil, a chopped onion, a teaspoon of chopped parsley and salt and pepper. Allow to brown a little then cover with stock or cold water and cook slowly for 2½ hours in a covered pan. An hour before serving time, by which time the broth will be somewhat reduced, make up to the original quantity by adding tomato sauce (see page 217).

MANZO IN UMIDO ALLA TRIESTINA
Stewed beef as cooked in Trieste

a piece of lean stewing
beef about 2 lb. in
weight
3 cloves
salt and pepper
1 oz. butter
stock

2 rashers streaky
bacon
1 onion, 2 stalks of
celery and 1 carrot
chopped small
white wine

Make holes in the beef with the point of a sharp knife and push strips of the streaky bacon into them; season with salt and pepper, and place in a stewpan with the butter, cloves and vegetables, and allow to brown; then cover with stock and white wine in the proportions of 2 to 1, and cook slowly with the lid on the stewpan for 2½ or 3 hours. At the end of that time, remove the meat to a hot dish, skim the fat off the gravy and pour over the meat.

MANZO IN UMIDO
Stewed Beef

2 or 3 lb. stewing beef, *not* cut in pieces	1 onion
2 slices streaky bacon	2 sticks celery } all cut small
1 tablespoon tomato conserve diluted with a little broth	1 carrot
	beef marrow if available
	meat stock
salt and pepper	1 oz. butter
	nutmeg

With the point of a sharp knife make several small holes in the piece of beef and into these stuff strips of streaky bacon; season with pepper, salt and nutmeg.

Having prepared your piece of meat in this fashion, place it in a stewpan with about 1 oz. butter, a little beef marrow if available, and the chopped vegetables and allow to brown slowly, turning the meat so that it browns on all sides; then add meat stock nearly to cover it. Cover the stewpan and cook over slow heat for 2½ or 3 hours. When half cooked, add the tomato conserve diluted with some of the broth, and continue cooking till the meat is tender, by which time the broth should be reduced in quantity and thickened. Serve in a dish, surrounded by the broth.

COSCIA DI MANZO ALLA CASALINGA
Rump steak housewife fashion

Take a piece of rump steak, and 'lard' it by pricking with the point of a sharp knife and pushing strips of fat bacon into the incisions; season with pepper, salt and nutmeg, and wrap in 2 or 3 slices of fat ham or bacon. Place in a casserole with a chopped onion, ½ pint meat stock and 2 tablespoons white wine and allow to cook slowly in a moderate oven for 2½ or 3 hours.

STUFATO ALLA FIORENTINA

Stew as cooked in Florence

2 lb. stewing beef cut in pieces for serving	1 teaspoon chopped rosemary
2 tablespoons olive oil	1½ tablespoons red wine
3 cloves of garlic, crushed	1 tablespoon tomato conserve

Heat the oil and in it allow the garlic and rosemary to brown before adding the meat; allow the meat also to brown, then reduce heat and add red wine, and the tomato conserve diluted with a similar quantity of meat stock or water. Cover the pan and cook slowly for 2½ hours, adding more hot stock or boiling water from time to time if the meat looks like becoming dry.

If liked, potatoes peeled and cut in pieces may be added to the stewpan an hour before serving, so that they absorb the flavour of the meat as they cook.

Veal

If you are buying veal for 'escalopes', you need thin slices of the lean meat cut from the leg or from the fillet, and if you are not the possessor of a 'cutlet bat', remember to ask your butcher to flatten the escalopes for you with his cleaver; this type of rough treatment means a far more tender finished dish, and an escalope, remember, should be tender enough almost to melt in the mouth when eaten.

It's as well to be extravagant when cooking veal, using butter for frying, rather than dripping; butter costs a little more, but the flavour is lighter and far more delicious when veal is fried crisp in good butter.

COSTOLETTE or SCALOPPE MILANESE

Either a cutlet or an escalope of veal may be cooked *alla Milanese*. In either case allow 1 or 1½ per person, depending upon the size, and before starting to cook, either flatten the meat yourself with a cutlet bat, or have the butcher flatten it for you.

If you want to be truly Milanese, you will allow your meat to marinate in a bath of milk for an hour or so before starting to cook it, but this refinement may be omitted without any real detriment to the finished dish.

Remove all fat and gristle.

Coat your cutlets or escalopes in beaten egg which has been seasoned with salt and pepper; allow surplus egg to drip off, then dip the meat in fine toasted breadcrumbs before frying it on both sides in a generous amount of hot butter. Cook quickly on one side until golden, then turn and cook the other, and lift out of the pan with a perforated slice so that any surplus fat goes back into the pan. Serve with quartered lemons and a garnish of parsley.

You may either serve these hot, with a green salad, or having drained them well, and allowed them to cool, they are equally delicious served cold.

SCALOPPE or COSTOLETTE DI VITELLO AL SUGO

Prepare your escalopes as for *Scaloppe alla Milanese* then arrange them in a flat fireproof dish, and over them pour hot tomato sauce (see page 217) which will be all the better if when making it you have added a bay leaf.

Serve hot, with a green salad.

SCALOPPINE AL MARSALA

The combination of thin, crisply fried pieces of veal with Marsala is an experiment well worth trying.

Scaloppine, known sometimes by the name of *piccate*, are much smaller than escalopes; they are cut very thin and should not be much more than 2 inches square. 3 or 4 per person is the usual allowance.

Beat your scaloppine flat, and flour them with flour that has been seasoned with pepper and salt. In a frying pan large enough to accommodate them, if possible, in one layer, heat a fairly generous knob of butter, and when it is really hot, brown the scaloppine very quickly on each side. While they are still in the pan, add about a tablespoon of Marsala for every 4 scaloppine, and bring to a bubbling oil; add a teaspoon of chicken stock for each tablespoon of Marsala; stir well, and allow to cook for a few moments under a lower heat. Remember that one essential of this dish is *quick* cooking; altogether the process should take under 10 minutes.

Serve very hot.

SCALOPPE ALLA MODENESE

Allow 1 or 1½ escalopes per person; flatten them with a cutlet bat, coat with egg and breadcrumbs and fry in hot butter. Then place the escalopes side by side in a flat fireproof dish, and on top of each place a slice of ham, and on top of that a thin slice of Gruyère cheese. Place in a hot oven, and serve immediately the cheese has melted.

VITELLO TONNATO
Veal with Tunny Fish

Remove the skin and fat from a piece of leg of veal; remove the bone, and stick the meat with small fillets of anchovy. Tie it firmly and allow it to boil for 1½ hours in a saucepan, covered completely with water in which have been placed a small onion, 2 cloves, a bay leaf, a little chopped celery, parsley and salt. At the end of this time, lift the meat from the water — reserving the broth to form the basis of a minestrone. Untie the meat, cut it in slices and place in a dish covered with the following sauce, in which it should be left for 2 days, after which it should be served cold, with the sauce served in a separate vessel.

SAUCE FOR VITELLO TONNATO

Mince the contents of a 4-oz. tin of tunny fish with 2 anchovies, and pass through a sieve or a food mill, adding olive oil and lemon juice in the proportions of 3 parts of oil to 1 of lemon juice, and finally adding a few chopped capers.

VITELLO IN UMIDO CON PISELLI
Veal stew with peas

2 lb. lean veal	butter or oil for
meat stock and/or	browning
tomato sauce (see	8 oz. fresh green peas
page 217)	(weighed after shelling)

Heat a little butter or oil in a stewpan, and in it brown the veal, which has been cut into 2-inch pieces. Add several tablespoonfuls of hot stock and/or tomato sauce, cover and cook gently for 30 minutes, adding a little more stock if it looks like drying out; add the peas, and simmer gently for a further 1½ hours.

BRACIUOLE DI VITELLO ALLA VERONESE
Veal chops in the Veronese style

Allow one chop per person, and while these are being grilled, prepare the following sauce:

2 cloves garlic
1 tablespoon chopped
   parsley

2 or 3 anchovies from
   which bones have
   been removed
2 oz. butter

Pound together all the ingredients except the butter in a mortar until a paste is formed, then add the butter and cream well together. Pour into the dish in which the chops are to be served, and keep hot over a saucepan of boiling water. When the chops are cooked, arrange in the dish and serve hot with sections of lemon.

VITELLO IN FRICASSEA
Fricassée of veal

Cut lean veal into small pieces. Fry an onion until golden brown in a little butter; add the pieces of veal and brown on all sides; cover with boiling stock, lower the heat and allow to cook until about half the liquid is evaporated (about 30 minutes). Meanwhile, beat 2 or 3 egg yolks with the juice of a ½ lemon and a little chopped parsley, and when the veal has finished cooking, add the egg and lemon mixture, removing the stewpan from the heat so as not to curdle the eggs. Mix well and serve hot.

ROAST VEAL

Allow about 30 minutes to the pound in a very moderate oven (300° F.). Pound together a clove of garlic and an anchovy, and rub these over the roast of veal before cooking. Cover the meat with strips of fat bacon or salt pork to prevent its drying out, and cook in a casserole with a little butter. Be careful if you are salting it not to overdo this, as the anchovy will have made it fairly salty. At the end of the cooking, add 3 tablespoons red wine to the gravy, and baste the veal with this before removing from the oven.

OSSOBUCO ALLA MILANESE

TO SERVE 4

allow one small knuckle of veal per person, and it should be sawn nearly through in sections about 1½ or 2 inches long, so that one has a number of sections of bone, each surrounded by a circle of muscle

flour
2 or 3 oz. butter
salt and pepper
1 gill dry white wine
1 tablespoon chopped parsley
1 anchovy
grated rind of ½ lemon
stock or water
1 clove garlic

Heat the butter in a heavy pan large enough to accommodate the veal knuckles in one layer; flour the knuckles and brown on both sides in the hot butter, seasoning with salt and pepper; add the wine, and continue cooking until the wine has almost evaporated, then add stock or water just to cover the meat; cover closely, and cook slowly for at least 1 hour, adding more stock if it looks as though the meat is drying. Meanwhile pound together in a mortar the garlic, anchovy, lemon rind and parsley, and 5 minutes before serving, add to the gravy, and bring to the boil, stirring with a wooden spoon.

It is customary to serve Ossobuco with a plain Risotto, coloured with saffron; this, incidentally, is the only instance of rice served *with* a meat dish.

AGNELLO ARROSTO
Roast Lamb

Try roasting a leg of lamb Italian fashion. Before putting it in the oven, make a slit in the flesh near the bone and into this place 1 or 2 cloves of garlic and a sprig of rosemary. Oil the meat lightly all over, and place in a hot oven, allowing 15 minutes to the pound and 15 minutes over, and basting from time to time with oil, and, to make it even more delicious, 15 minutes before serving, pour over it 3 tablespoons white wine and baste finally with the juices that have run into the roasting pan.

AGNELLO O CAPRETTO IN CASSERUOLA
Lamb or Kid Pot Roast

Kid is eaten a great deal in Italy and the flesh of young goats makes excellent eating. Try a leg of either kid or lamb stuck at intervals with rosemary, salted, and then browned on all sides in a stewpan in which 2 tablespoons olive oil have been heated. Cover the stewpan when the flesh is browned on all sides, and allow it to cook slowly, 15 minutes to the pound, in the steam that will develop in the stewpan once it is covered.

SAUSAGES WITH TOMATO SAUCE
TO SERVE 4

1 lb. pure pork sausages	chopped sage
olive oil	tomato sauce (see page 217)

Puncture the sausages, then fry in the olive oil to which a teaspoon of chopped sage has been added; when they are browned, cover with tomato sauce. Cover pan and cook gently for 20 minutes. The sage may be omitted if the flavour is not liked.

SALSICCIE ALLA TRIESTINA

Sausages as cooked in Trieste

TO SERVE 4]

1 lb. pure pork sausages	2 tablespoons grated Parmesan
1 gill white wine	1 gill meat stock

Puncture the sausages, then place in a saucepan with stock and white wine and cook gently on the top of the stove for about 20 minutes; at the end of that time, add the Parmesan cheese, stir well, and serve very hot.

PORK COOKED IN MILK 'ALLA BOLOGNESE'

For this you need a piece of loin of pork, boned and with some of its fat removed. If you are going to cook it in the true Bolognese manner, you will prepare it overnight by sprinkling with salt and pepper and leaving till morning, but this treatment is not essential if time is at a premium.

If you are preparing the meat the day you are cooking, sprinkle it with salt and black pepper before rolling it up, and it is an improvement if a clove of garlic is sliced thin and rolled up in the centre of the meat, together with a few seeds of coriander or fennel.

Use a saucepan that is more or less the size of the rolled joint, and when the pork is ready for the pan, heat a little butter in it and brown the pork all over.

Heat the milk, allowing roughly a pint of milk to each pound of pork, and pour over the meat. Cover the saucepan and allow to simmer gently for an hour or a little longer; uncover, and allow to cook for another 30 minutes, by which time the quantity of liquid will be reduced considerably, and it should be a golden brown in colour. Take care that the saucepan does not go dry; if there is any danger of this, add a little more hot milk. The joint is excellent hot, served with the sauce from the cooking, and if you are able to add a few sliced truffles to this it is all the better. Another addition is that of a chopped onion and a rasher of bacon cut in small pieces, and cooked in the butter before the pork is browned.

LOIN OF PORK
as cooked in Tuscany

Again your loin pork should be boned and some of its fat
should be removed before cooking, and before rolling it
should be stuck with a few rosemary leaves and a few slivers
of garlic, and seasoned with salt and pepper. Roll and tie it
and roast in the oven in the usual fashion, allowing 25 to
30 minutes per pound, plus 25 or 30 minutes over. This is
excellent allowed to cool and served with a potato salad.

And as cooked in Perugia

Here, instead of rosemary, fennel leaves are used, and when
the meat is cooked and served cold, it is a good touch to
serve with it a potato salad with which has been mixed
a little thinly sliced fennel.

PORK CHOPS 'ALLA NAPOLITANA'
TO SERVE 4

The Neapolitans use a lot of green and red and yellow peppers
in their cooking, and these 'marry' well with pork. For this
recipe take:

6 pork chops	8 oz. mushrooms
2 red or yellow peppers	oil for cooking
1 tablespoon tomato	salt and pepper
paste	1 clove garlic, crushed

Heat oil in a heavy pan, fry garlic in it till pale brown, add the
chops and brown on both sides; add salt and pepper. Remove
from the pan and keep warm. Meanwhile, dilute the tomato
paste with a little water and add to the pan in which the
chops have been cooked, remove the seeds and stem from
the peppers and chop them finely, and add these to the pan
together with the chopped mushrooms; cover and cook slowly
for about 15 minutes, then replace the chops, cooking together for another 20 minutes or so. Serve very hot.

PORK CHOPS WITH PRUNES

TO SERVE 6

6 pork chops	oil or butter for frying
salt and pepper	2 tablespoons white wine

Heat the oil with the pepper and salt in a stewpan and in it fry the chops first on one side and then on the other until brown, add the wine and cook over slightly lowered heat until the wine has evaporated, then remove the chops to a hot dish and cover with the following sauce.

SAUCE

1 onion	2 slices lean ham
1 oz. butter	2 tablespoons wine
10 or a dozen prunes	vinegar
which have been	salt
soaked in water	chopped thyme
until softened	bay leaf

Soak the prunes, and when soft remove the stones. Fry the chopped onion and ham cut in small pieces in butter until light brown, add the vinegar, and cook until the sauce is reduced by one half. Place the prunes in a small saucepan, with barely enough water to cover them, a pinch of chopped thyme and a bay leaf and cook slowly till soft. Pass through a sieve or food mill and add to the chopped onion and ham; mix well and pour over the pork chops.

FEGATO ALLA SPAGNOLA

Liver as served in Spain

TO SERVE 6

1½ lb. calf's liver
2 large onions sliced
thinly into rings
sprigs of parsley
flour

1 dozen small firm
tomatoes
1 lemon
oil
salt and pepper

Heat the grill, and meanwhile, dip the liver — sliced to about ½ inch thickness — in the flour, then into oil, and grill first on one side then on the other. Set on one side to keep warm, and having seasoned the tomatoes with salt, pepper and oil, grill these also. While this is going on, fry the onions until a golden yellow. Have ready a large flat dish, and pile the onions into a pyramid in the centre, with the slices of liver around, garnished with grilled tomatoes and sprigs of parsley, and the lemon cut into sections.

FEGATO ALL' ITALIANA

Liver in the Italian style

TO SERVE 6

1½ lb. calf's liver, cut
into thin slices
2 oz. butter

flour
pepper and salt
1 lemon

Heat the butter very hot in a large heavy frying pan. Flour the slices of liver and fry quickly, first on one side and then on the other, the whole process to take not more than 5 or 6 minutes. Season with pepper and salt, add a small knob of butter, and shake the pan well so that it is distributed over the slices of liver. Remove the pan from the fire, and sprinkle the liver with the juice of ½ lemon before removing to a hot dish for serving. Serve very hot.

Having tried out these two fairly conservative methods of cooking liver, how about trying a Tuscan speciality? See the next page for an easy recipe.

FEGATO ALLA TOSCANA

TO SERVE 6

1½ lb. calf's liver cut
  into thin slices
flour
oil
pepper and salt

1 good tablespoon of
  fresh sage leaves
  chopped small
1 lemon, cut into
  sections

Flour the liver, and fry in hot oil very quickly; before removing from the stove, season with pepper and salt, and the sage leaves cut small. Serve very hot accompanied by sections of lemon.

Or, having enjoyed veal escalopes *alla Milanese*, why not try liver treated similarly?

FEGATO ALLA MILANESE

TO SERVE 6

1½ lb. calf's liver,
  cut into thin slices
flour
pepper and salt
1 tablespoon chopped
  parsley

1 beaten egg
breadcrumbs
butter for frying
1 lemon

For this recipe start preparations 1¼ hours before you wish to serve the dish, for the slices of liver are spread on a flat dish, seasoned with salt, pepper and the chopped parsley and left to 'mind their own business' for a good hour. At the end of this time, heat the butter in a heavy pan; flour the liver, then dip in beaten egg, and then into crisp breadcrumbs, and fry quickly first on one side and then on the other. Arrange on a flat, heated dish, pour over the liver the remainder of the butter in which it was fried, and garnish with sections of lemon and sprigs of parsley.

In Venice the method is strongly reminiscent of 'liver and onions', except that oil is used for cooking whereas we normally use lard or dripping. See the next page for a recipe for liver cooked the Venetian way.

FEGATO ALLA VENEZIANA

For each person allow about 4 oz. liver and 1 large onion cut into rings. Heat the oil in a heavy pan and in it cook the onions until they are a golden yellow; add the liver — floured — and cook quickly on either side, season with salt and pepper and serve piled upon a bed of the fried onions.

For real luxury, why not try liver cooked with artichokes? Since globe artichokes are not always easy to obtain in this country, you may have to make do with the bottled or tinned variety, well drained.

LIVER WITH ARTICHOKES

For each person allow 4 oz. calf's liver, and 1 or 2 artichokes.

In a heavy pan fry a chopped onion in a little oil until it is golden brown; lower the heat and add the artichokes divided into sections, and cook slowly for 20 minutes or so until the artichokes are tender; increase the heat, add the floured liver and cook quickly on first one side then the other; remove from the heat, season with salt, pepper and 1 tablespoon finely chopped parsley; sprinkle with lemon juice, and shake the pan well so that liver and artichokes are impregnated with the seasonings and lemon juice. Serve on a hot dish.

TUSCAN PIG'S LIVER

Here is an excellent way of serving pig's liver as prepared in Tuscany. There it is customary to serve the liver thus treated on a skewer, interspersed with small sections of toast, and bay leaves, but since grilling on a skewer is not the easiest way of cooking with modern appliances, omit the toast and the bay leaves, and having dipped your thin slices of pig's liver in beaten egg, dip them in the following mixture so that they are completely coated with it, and fry quickly in hot oil, then serve with sections of lemon.

MIXTURE FOR COATING

1—2 oz. crisp breadcrumbs   1 teaspoon fennel seeds
1 clove garlic, chopped   salt and pepper

Mix well together and when the liver has been dipped in
beaten egg, coat with this mixture before frying in hot oil.

FLAN DI FEGATO

8 oz. calves' liver or   1 oz. butter
  chicken livers   2 oz. salt pork
1 slice ham   1 or 2 truffles or ½ oz.
pinch spice   dried mushrooms
2 slices bread soaked   (soaked in water for
  in stock and squeezed   10 minutes)
  dry

Pass all ingredients through a mincer and add 2 tablespoons
Marsala, 2 tablespoons stock, 2 whole eggs and 1 additional
yolk; mix well and place in a greased soufflé dish and cook
in a moderate oven for 20 or 30 minutes.

POLPETTE DI FEGATO

Liver rissoles

8 oz. calves' liver   2 egg yolks
1 slice fat pork   salt and pepper
2 slices bread soaked in   flour
  stock and squeezed dry oil for frying
3 tablespoons grated   chopped onion
  Parmesan   white wine

Pound liver, pork and bread to a pulp with pestle and mortar,
then add cheese, salt and pepper to taste and beaten eggs
and form into small rissoles the size of a walnut. Sprinkle
with flour and fry in a *soffritto* of oil and chopped onion.
Sprinkle with a little white wine when half cooked.

Brain rissoles

brains as prepared for *Testa di Vitello alla Toscana* (see page 159)	beaten egg pepper and salt

Having prepared the brains as in the following recipe, allow to cook and then chop fine and bind together with the beaten egg; stir over the fire in a small pan until the mixture thickens but does not boil; allow to cook and then form into small rissoles, which fry in hot oil or butter after coating with egg and fine breadcrumbs. Serve with sections of lemon.

TESTA DI VITELLO ALLA TOSCANA

Brains as cooked in Tuscany

TO SERVE 4

calves' brains	juice of $\frac{1}{2}$ lemon
1 oz. butter	1 carrot
1 small onion	1 stalk celery
1 tablespoon parsley, chopped	salt and pepper

Wash the brains in salt and water, removing the skin and fibres and allow to remain in salt and water for 30 minutes or longer. Wrap in a piece of muslin and tie with string and put on to cook in a stewpan with water to cover and the chopped vegetables, seasoning and lemon juice, and cook for a further 15 or 20 minutes, or until the brains are firm; remove from the stewpan, untie, and serve on a hot dish with a piquant sauce.

ROGNONI IN UMIDO

Stewed kidneys

TO SERVE 4

    1 lb. calves' or sheep's kidneys
    1½ oz. butter
    ½ pint white wine

    1 teaspoon chopped parsley
    ½ lemon
    1 small onion

The kidneys must be skinned, cut in halves and the core removed; after this plunge them in boiling water to which juice of the lemon has been added. After 2 or 3 minutes, drain them and cut in slices. Heat the butter in a stewpan, and in it cook the chopped onion until light brown, add the kidneys and cook them for 5 or 6 minutes, shaking the pan from time to time to prevent sticking, add the wine and a little grated lemon rind, and allow the dish to bubble so that the gravy is reduced in volume; finally, a few minutes before serving, add the parsley. Serve hot in a dish surrounded by snippets of toast.

ROGNONI ALLA BOLOGNESE

Kidneys as cooked in Bologna

TO SERVE 4

    1 lb. calves' or pigs' kidneys
    2 oz. butter
    juice of ½ lemon

    2 medium sized onions
    ¼ pint stock
    1 tablespoon chopped parsley

Skin the kidneys, cut in half, removing the core, then plunge in boiling water to which a little vinegar or lemon juice has been added and leave for 2 or 3 minutes. Drain and cut in slices. Heat the butter in a stewpan and in it fry the chopped onion until golden brown and add the parsley; add the chopped kidneys and cook for 5 or 6 minutes, shaking the pan so that they are cooked on all sides and do not stick; finally, add the stock and a little lemon juice and cook gently for a further 10 minutes, but do not allow to boil.

LINGUA CON OLIVE

Tongue with olives

TO SERVE 4

1 calf's tongue
1 carrot chopped
1 oz. butter
½ pint boiling stock

1 small chopped onion
6 large green olives
salt

Put the tongue in a stewpan, cover with cold water to which a little salt has been added; boil for 1½ hours, then drain, cool and skin. Melt the butter in a stewpan and in it brown the chopped vegetables; add the tongue and brown all over, then add the stock and the olives cut in small pieces, cover and allow to cook gently for a further 1½ hours, adding a little more stock from time to time if necessary.

LINGUA ALLA SALSA

Tongue with sauce

TO SERVE 8

1 calf's tongue
1 lb. rump steak
1 teaspoon chopped
    basil
½ pint stock
2 slices streaky bacon

1 medium sized onion
1 teaspoon chopped
    parsley
1 bay leaf
4 oz. mushrooms
salt and pepper

Put the tongue in a stewpan with salted water to cover and bring to the boil, then simmer gently for at least 1½ hours. Drain, cool and remove the skin; puncture it here and there and into the holes introduce slivers of the streaky bacon. Grease a stewpan and in it place the steak, well beaten with a cutlet bat, then the chopped onion, basil, parsley, bay leaf and mushrooms cut small; on this lay the tongue, and cover with the other half of the steak, well beaten, and over it pour the stock. Cover the saucepan and allow to cook very slowly for about 3 hours, adding more stock if necessary during that time, but allowing the broth to reduce almost to nothing by the end of the cooking period. Serve hot with a piquant sauce, or cold with a green salad.

TRIPPA ALL'ITALIANA

Tripe, Italian fashion

TO SERVE 4

1 lb. tripe
1 clove garlic
1 dessertspoon flour
1 pint stock
1 teaspoon chopped basil
salt and pepper
bay leaf

1 large onion
4 tablespoons olive oil
2 medium tomatoes, peeled
1 carrot
1 stalk celery
1 teaspoon chopped parsley

Heat the oil and in it fry the chopped onion and crushed garlic until they are golden brown and then stir in the flour. Cut the washed tripe into squares, and add to the mixture, together with the tomatoes peeled and cut small. Slowly add the stock, stirring to prevent sticking to bottom of pan; add diced celery and carrot and seasoning. Allow to simmer gently for 1½ hours. Serve hot, removing the bay leaf before serving.

TRIPPA ALLA FIORENTINA

Tripe, Florentine style

TO SERVE 4

1 lb. tripe
pepper and salt, to taste
2 tablespoons Parmesan cheese

½ pint tomato sauce (see page 217)
1 teaspoon chopped marjoram

Cut the tripe into squares and boil for 30 minutes in boiling, salted water. Drain, then place in a stewpan with the tomato sauce and allow to simmer gently for a further hour; 15 minutes before serving, sprinkle in the marjoram, and when dished up, scatter the grated cheese over it, or hand it in a separate dish to be added at will.

TRIPE WITH PARMESAN

TO SERVE 4

1 lb. tripe	3 tablespoons Parmesan
2 oz. butter	cheese grated

Cut the tripe into small squares and cook in boiling, salted water for 1½ hours or until tender; drain, and reheat with the butter. When hot, stir in the Parmesan cheese and serve as soon as this starts to melt.

Stuffed Meats

BRACIUOLE RIPIENE

Stuffed steak

TO SERVE 4

For the filling:

about 2 lb. veal steak cut in thin layers and flattened with a cutlet bat

about 2 oz. of streaky bacon or lean ham	2 slices of bread, soaked in milk or water and squeezed dry
1 or 2 cloves of garlic, crushed	
1 teaspoon chopped parsley	1 egg yolk
2 oz. grated Parmesan cheese	a pinch of nutmeg
	salt and pepper

Chop the ham in small pieces, and to it add the other ingredients and mix well.

Cut the steak into strips about 7 inches in length and 3 inches in width, and on each spread a portion of the filling; roll the steak round the filling and fasten with thread.

In a heavy pan heat about 2 oz. butter, and, if available, a little marrow from a bone, and in this place the rolls of steak, and allow to brown on all sides; add a chopped onion, a finely chopped carrot and a stalk of celery cut small; cover pan and allow to cook together for 20 minutes, adding, towards the end of the cooking time, a few tablespoons of good stock or strained tomato sauce.

163

VITELLO RIPIENO AL PASTICCIO
Stuffed veal pie
TO SERVE 4

For the stuffing:

about 4 oz. lean veal
4 oz. veal sweetbreads
4 oz. lean ham
1 small onion chopped
small
2 oz. uncooked green
peas

a pinch of marjoram
1 oz. butter
1 egg and 3 extra yolks
1 tablespoon chopped
parsley
4 oz. mushrooms cut
small

Heat the butter, and in it cook the onion until it is a golden colour; then add the veal, sweetbreads and ham, cut small, and cook together for 10 or 12 minutes; remove from the stove and chop finely, then add the other ingredients.

Having prepared the above stuffing, take about 1½ lb. lean veal, cut in thin slices and pounded with a cutlet bat. Place a layer in a greased fireproof casserole, and on this place a layer of the stuffing, then a further layer of veal, and continue in this way till all is used up, finishing with a layer of veal; dot with butter, and bake in a moderate oven for 45 minutes, basting from time to time with a little good stock or strained tomato sauce. This may be eaten hot or cold.

Poultry and Game

Chicken

POLLO IN UMIDO
Chicken stew
TO SERVE 4

1 medium sized boiling
  fowl
1 stalk celery, cut small
1 teaspoon chopped
  parsley
1 tablespoon tomato
  conserve

4 oz. mushrooms
1 small onion, chopped
1 carrot, chopped
1 oz. butter
½ pint stock or water
pepper and salt

Clean and prepare the fowl and cut into joints for serving.
Heat the butter in a stewpan and in it cook the chopped
vegetables a few minutes; add the chicken and brown on all
sides, then add the stock, the mushrooms cut small, and the
tomato conserve diluted with a little stock or water. Cover the
pan and simmer gently for 2 hours or until the chicken is
tender, adding a little more stock if necessary during the
cooking time.

POLLO ALLE OLIVE
Chicken with olives
TO SERVE 4

In addition to the ingredients for *Pollo in Umido* in the preceding recipe, you will need 6 or 8 large green olives. Proceed
as in the preceding recipe but do not cut the fowl into joints,
but leave it whole. After adding the stock, add the olives,
stoned and cut in strips; allow the pan to simmer for 2 hours
or until the chicken is tender, then serve on a heated dish
with the sauce served in a separate tureen.

POLLO CON VERDURE

Garnished chicken

TO SERVE 4

1 medium sized boiling fowl	8 oz. pork sausages
1 small onion, chopped small	2 slices streaky bacon
	1 oz. butter
1 level tablespoon flour	½ pint stock or water
1 tablespoon tomato conserve	1 carrot
	1 small cabbage
2 stalks celery	salt, pepper and nutmeg

Clean the fowl and cut in pieces for serving. Place the butter in a stewpan, heat it and in it cook the chopped onion till it is golden brown; add the pieces of chicken and allow to brown on all sides; stir in the flour and allow to cook a moment or two before adding the stock very slowly, stirring so as to prevent lumps forming; add the salt, pepper and nutmeg, the carrot and celery cut small; cover and cook slowly for 2 hours or until the chicken is tender; 20 minutes before serving, add the cabbage, washed and shredded, and the sausages, and when these are cooked, serve in a heated dish.

POLLO AI PISELLI

Chicken with peas

Prepare as for *Pollo ai Funghi* (see page 167), but instead of the mushrooms add 1 lb. fresh green peas — weighed after shelling — and a tablespoon of chopped parsley to the broth after the chicken is nearly cooked, and when the peas are cooked, serve the whole in a hot dish.

POLLO ALLA CREMA

Chicken with cream

TO SERVE 4

    1 medium sized roasting   flour
       fowl   1 tablespoon or more
    1 small onion   butter
    1 gill cream or 'top of
       the milk'

Prepare the fowl, cut in pieces for serving. Heat the butter and in it brown the onion; then flour the pieces of chicken and cook on all sides in the heated butter, salting to taste. Add the cream and allow to cook to boiling point; remove from the stove and serve sprinkled with chopped parsley.

POLLO AI FUNGHI

Chicken with mushrooms

TO SERVE 4

    1 medium sized boiling   2 oz. butter
       chicken   ½ pint stock or water
    1 small onion   4 oz. mushrooms
    1 tablespoon tomato   salt
       conserve   flour

Prepare the chicken for cooking and cut in pieces. Heat the butter in a stewpan and in it cook the chopped onion until yellow. Lightly flour the chicken and fry in the butter until brown on all sides; salt to taste and add the stock and the tomato conserve diluted with a little stock. Cover and cook slowly for 2 hours or until the chicken is tender; lift the chicken from the gravy, and keep hot; meanwhile, clean the mushrooms and cut small, add them to the gravy and cook for 10 minutes, then return the chicken to the stewpan, and when it has been in the gravy long enough for it to have come to the boil, serve in a hot dish.

PETTI DI POLLO ALLA LOMBARDA

Chicken breasts Lombardy style

TO SERVE 4

2 chicken breasts
1 small onion
1 tablespoon chopped
  fennel
1 or 2 chicken livers
1 oz. butter

1 teaspoon chopped
  parsley
1 lb. shelled green peas
½ pint hot stock or water
juice of ½ lemon
2 egg yolks
salt and pepper

Heat the butter in a stewpan and in it brown the chopped onion and parsley; add the chicken, lightly floured, and brown on all sides, add the chopped fennel and the hot stock, cover and allow to cook for 25 minutes. Meanwhile cook the peas in boiling salted water for 10 minutes, drain and add to the stewpan together with the chicken livers and seasoning; cook for a further 10 minutes, then remove from the stove and stir in the beaten egg yolks mixed with the lemon juice. Serve immediately.

POLLO AL VINO BIANCO

Chicken with white wine

TO SERVE 4

1 boiling fowl
1 gill white wine
1 tablespoon olive oil
pinch nutmeg
salt to taste

butter
½ pint stock
flour
chopped parsley

Prepare fowl and cut in pieces, then lay on a flat dish and allow to marinate for at least 4 hours in mixed wine, olive oil, salt and nutmeg. Turn from time to time. Then remove chicken, place in a stewpan with a little butter and the stock, and cook slowly for at least 2 hours, finally thickening the broth with a little flour mixed with a little cold water, stirred into the stewpan and allowed to thicken, stirring all the time. Finally add a little chopped parsley and serve hot.

CHICKEN AS SERVED IN ROME

TO SERVE 4

1 medium sized boiling
 fowl
4 tablespoons olive oil
1 sliced leek
a pinch of thyme
1 tablespoon tomato
 conserve

2 oz. flour
4 cloves
a little chopped parsley
1 pint stock
4 oz. macaroni
salt and pepper

Heat the oil in a large stewpan, and having prepared the chicken, add it to the stewpan with the chopped leek, cloves, herbs; allow it to brown on all sides, and take your time over this process. Pour off half the oil. Add the stock and the tomato conserve diluted with a little stock or water; cover and allow to finish cooking — at least another 1½ to 2 hours until the chicken is tender. Meanwhile cook and drain the macaroni, and when the chicken has finished cooking, remove it from the sauce and keep hot; add the macaroni to the sauce, mix well and serve around the chicken as a garnish.

PURÉE OF CHICKEN

TO SERVE 4

breast of 1 medium
 sized chicken
2 slices bread
stock
2 tablespoons Marsala
pinch mixed spice

2 tablespoons brown
 sauce (see page 215)
1 egg yolk
juice of ½ lemon
salt and pepper
fried bread

Pound chicken meat in a mortar with a little stock and the bread which you have soaked in stock and squeezed dry. When well mixed, pass through a food mill, place in a stewpan with Marsala, brown sauce and mixed spice. Cook gently for 20 minutes, then remove from heat and mix with beaten egg yolk and lemon juice; season with salt and pepper to taste and serve on a dish surrounded by snippets of hot fried bread.

Game

HARE IN SWEET SOUR SAUCE

TO SERVE 4

1 hare	salt
vinegar	2 tablespoons sugar
3 oz. butter	2 teaspoons grated
1 chopped onion	bitter chocolate
1 slice ham	1 tablespoon chopped
stock	fennel
flour	seedless raisins

Skin and clean hare, cut in pieces, wash in a weak solution of vinegar and water and flour lightly. Fry in butter, in which you have browned the chopped onion and the ham cut in small squares. Cover with stock and salt to taste and cook slowly in a covered stewpan for about 1½ hours. Meanwhile mix together the sugar with 2 tablespoons vinegar, bitter chocolate, fennel and raisins, and add this mixture to the hare 20 minutes before serving.

HARE STEW

TO SERVE 4

1 hare	1 slice ham
1 oz. butter	flour
2 tablespoons olive oil	1 gill white wine
1 chopped onion	1 tablespoon tomato
1 clove garlic crushed	conserve
pinch rosemary	½ pint stock
1 stalk celery	½ oz. dried mushrooms
pinch nutmeg	soaked in water

Heat butter and oil in a heavy stewpan and brown chopped onion in it. Add celery chopped fine, garlic, rosemary and ham. Cook together for several minutes then add hare cut in pieces, washed and lightly floured, and brown. Then slowly add wine, tomato conserve, stock, mushrooms and nutmeg. Cover and cook gently for 1½ to 2 hours.

PIGEONS WITH PEAS

Allow 1 pigeon per person, and when cleaned, brown them all over in a stewpan in hot butter to which has been added a chopped onion. Salt to taste and cover with boiling stock and a little tomato conserve diluted with stock or water. Cook gently for 1½ hours, then remove the pigeons and keep hot; meanwhile in the broth in which they have cooked, place 8 oz. shelled green peas to every 2 pigeons, cook for 20 minutes, then replace the pigeons, allow to cook together a few minutes and serve hot. A little chopped basil is a welcome addition to this dish.

PERNICIOTTE ALLA MILANESE
Young partridges as cooked in Milan

Pluck and draw the birds and cut in two, lengthways, and flatten slightly with a cutlet bat. Allow them to marinate for an hour before cooking, in oil seasoned with salt, pepper, a little parsley and a crushed bay leaf. Then, one half at a time, dip in crisp breadcrumbs and fry on both sides in hot olive oil. Arrange on a heated dish and serve with anchovy sauce (see page 234).

BECCACCE AL SALMI
Woodcock

These tender little birds need plucking very carefully, and the head, which is left on the body, is skinned. They are *not* drawn before cooking.

Partly cook the woodcock in a stewpan with a little oil seasoned with salt, then cut in two, and remove the inside, throwing away the stomach and gall, but using the remainder to enrich the salmi, or sauce. Having removed the birds from the pan, heat a little butter, and in it brown a chopped onion and the insides removed from the birds and cut in small pieces; replace the birds, adding a very little stock to prevent the birds drying; cover and cook until tender. Serve garnished with snippets of toast spread with the salmi.

BECCACCE ALLA ROMAGNOLA

Another way with woodcock

For this recipe, having plucked the bodies and skinned the heads, remove the insides. Throw away the stomach and the gall, and put the remaining insides in a mortar with a little butter, 4 thin slices of ham cut in small pieces, a little chopped parsley and a little soft breadcrumbs that have been soaked in water or milk and squeezed dry. Pound to a paste, season with pepper and salt and stuff the birds with the mixture, tying with thread or fine string, and twisting the head round so that the beak can be used as a skewer through the thighs. Wrap a piece of thin fat pork around the breast, sprinkle with salt, wrap in buttered paper and cook gently in a moderate oven for about an hour; remove the paper, dip the birds in beaten white of egg, sprinkle with crisp breadcrumbs and allow to cook for a further 15 minutes so as to give them some colour. Remove the string or thread and serve accompanied with piquant sauce (see page 220) and sections of lemon.

FAGIANO AL MADERA

Pheasant cooked in Madeira

TO SERVE 4

1 pheasant	2 oz. butter
4 rashers fat bacon	salt and pepper
2 slices ham	pinch of nutmeg
½ onion	1 gill Madeira
1 stick celery	1 gill stock
1 teaspoon chopped parsley	fried bread
1 carrot	

Pluck and draw pheasant. Melt butter in a stewpan and put in the pheasant with bacon, ham and onion cut small, finely chopped celery, parsley, diced carrot, salt, pepper and nutmeg. Cook together slowly until the pheasant begins to brown, then add Madeira and stock.

Cover the stewpan and allow about 45 minutes for the bird to finish cooking. Then place the pheasant in a hot dish, strain the fat from the sauce, pass through a sieve and pour over the bird. Serve garnished with croûtons of fried bread.

CONIGLIO IN SALSA PICCANTE

Rabbit in piquant sauce

TO SERVE 4

1 rabbit	3 cloves
flour	salt and pepper
2 oz. butter	pinch nutmeg
1 stick celery	1 gill red wine
1 teaspoon chopped parsley	1 gill stock
1 small onion	2 tablespoons capers
1 carrot	2 anchovies
4 oz. mushrooms	toast or fried bread

Skin rabbit, remove entrails and cut into joints. Flour lightly and place in a stewpan in which the butter has been melted. Brown on all sides, then add celery, parsley, onion and carrot, all chopped small, cloves, salt, pepper and nutmeg. Add wine and stock, cover pan and allow to cook for about 1 hour, then remove the pieces of rabbit and keep warm.

Pass gravy through a sieve, pressing it through with a wooden spoon so as not to leave anything behind but the dregs. Add capers and anchovies that have been pounded in a mortar; mix well, replace in the stewpan with the pieces of rabbit, and allow to boil for a few minutes more. Serve surrounded by croûtons of toast or fried bread.

FRICASSÉE OF RABBIT

Heat 1 oz. of butter in a stewpan, and in it fry a tablespoon of butter until brown, then add a rabbit, cut into joints and floured, together with a couple of slices of fat bacon cut small, and allow to cook until the rabbit has browned — say 15 minutes. Cover with a wineglass of white wine and an equal quantity of stock, add a chopped onion and a pinch of pepper, and cook fairly slowly until the liquid is reduced by half and the rabbit is tender. Remove the rabbit on to a hot dish, remove the pan from the fire and into the sauce mix the beaten yolks of two eggs and the juice of a ½ lemon. Mix well and pour over the rabbit before serving.

CONIGLIO ALLA BORGHESE
Rabbit 'Citizen' style
TO SERVE 4

1 rabbit	pinch thyme and
2 oz. butter	nutmeg
1 gill white wine	salt and pepper
1 onion	4 oz. fresh or ½ oz.
1 teaspoon chopped parsley	dried mushrooms

Skin rabbit and remove entrails. Cut into joints, wash and wipe dry, and place in stewpan in which butter has been melted. Brown on all sides, then lower heat and add white wine, chopped onion, parsley, thyme, nutmeg, salt, pepper and chopped mushrooms. If you are using dried mushrooms 'soak' first in a little stock or water. Cover stewpan and cook slowly for 1½ hours, adding a little stock from time to time if it looks as though the rabbit is drying out.

Where vegetables are concerned, the Italian cook is considerably more imaginative than her English counterpart, and one is unlikely to be confronted with 'plain boiled' potatoes, or with watery vegetable marrow served with a thin white sauce; try some of these suggestions for livening up the vegetable dishes.

CARCIOFI
Artichokes

Globe artichokes, a luxury in England, are one of Italy's staple vegetables. In Sicily one can pass acres and acres of land planted with these delicious vegetables; small wonder that they make frequent appearances on the Italian menu.

To prepare them for cooking, remove the outer leaves, cut off half of the top, or point of the artichoke, cut in halves and then in quarters, and allow to remain for about 30 minutes in water to which you have added a little lemon juice or vinegar. Drain and place in a saucepan with a little oil, a little lemon juice, salt, pepper, a clove of garlic, crushed, and a pinch of oregano, allow the artichokes to cook for 15 minutes, turning them frequently so that they become golden brown all over; remove to a hot dish and keep warm and to the sauce add one or two anchovies cut in small pieces, and cook together for a few minutes, then pour over the artichokes and serve hot.

CARCIOFI IN FRICASSEA
Fricassée of artichokes

Prepare the artichokes by removing the outer leaves, and cutting off half or a little more of the pointed end; leave for 30 minutes in water to which you have added a little lemon juice. Drain, and place in a saucepan with a little butter, chopped parsley, a clove of garlic crushed, and salt to taste. Allow to cook slowly for 45 minutes, then remove the pan from the heat, and add 1 or 2 egg yolks (depending on the quantity of artichokes) beaten lightly with a teaspoon of water per egg yolk, the juice of $\frac{1}{2}$ lemon, and 1 tablespoon grated Parmesan cheese. Serve very hot.

CARCIOFI IN UMIDO CON PISELLI

Artichokes stewed with peas
TO SERVE 4

12 globe artichokes	salt and pepper
12 oz. shelled fresh peas, weighed after shelling	1 small onion
	chopped parsley
	juice of ½ lemon
3 egg yolks	¼ pint stock or water
1 tablespoon olive oil	

Prepare the artichokes; meanwhile, chop the onion and fry lightly in the oil, together with the parsley; add the artichokes, quartered, the peas and the stock, together with pepper and salt. Cook together for 30 minutes, stirring from time to time so that the vegetables do not stick to the bottom of the pan; at the end of the cooking time, remove from the heat and stir in the beaten yolks of eggs and the lemon juice and serve hot.

CARCIOFI ALLA GIUDAICA

Jewish Artichokes
TO SERVE 4

Prepare a dozen artichokes, leaving a fairly long stem. While they are soaking, prepare a *battuto* with a little chopped parsley, a little chopped mint, a crushed clove of garlic, and place a little of this in the middle of each artichoke after draining the vegetable. In a deep pan heat ½ pint olive oil very hot and in this place the artichokes upside down, pressing them down so that the leaves spread out. Cook over a hot flame for 10 minutes and serve with sections of lemon.

ASPARAGI ALLA MILANESE

Asparagus Milanese Style

Having prepared and cooked your bundle of asparagus, drain, and lay in a fireproof dish, with a lump of butter, pepper and salt and place in a hot oven for a few moments; just before serving, sprinkle with 2 tablespoons grated Parmesan cheese, and serve as soon as this starts to melt.

ASPARAGI ALL'OLIO

Asparagus with oil

TO SERVE 4

Remove the hard end of the stalks of a bundle of asparagus, and remove the 'scales' that are to be found along the stalks; tie in smaller bundles with fine string and boil gently in salted water for about 20 minutes. Remove from the water, cut the string and remove, and serve with either melted butter or olive oil.

FAGIOLINI AL BURRO

Buttered French Beans

TO SERVE 4

1 lb. young French beans	2 tablespoons grated Parmesan
2 oz. butter	salt and pepper

Top and tail the beans, and cook them in boiling salted water for 20 minutes; drain, and place in a greased fireproof dish with the butter, pepper and salt and grated cheese, and place in a moderate oven until the cheese starts to melt. Serve immediately.

FAGIOLINI ALLA ROMANA

French beans, Roman style

TO SERVE 4

1 lb. young French beans	1 oz. butter
1 medium onion chopped small	salt, pepper and nutmeg
	2 anchovies cut small

Prepare the beans and boil in salted water for 15 minutes, saving a little of the cooking water, and drain. Place in a stewpan in which you have prepared a *battuto* of the butter, onion, seasonings and chopped anchovies, together with a little of the water in which the beans were cooked; cook gently for 10 minutes, during which time the liquid will have reduced in quantity. Remove from the fire and serve.

FAGIOLINI IN FRICASSEA

Fricassée of French Beans

TO SERVE 4

1 lb. French beans	2 oz. butter
1 tablespoon chopped parsley	salt and pepper
1 clove garlic, crushed	1 or 2 egg yolks, beaten lightly with 1 tea-
juice of ½ lemon	spoon cold water
1 tablespoon grated Parmesan	per yolk

Prepare the beans and cook in boiling salted water for 15 minutes, then drain, and place in a stewpan with the parsley, butter, garlic and salt; allow to cook gently for a further 10 minutes, remove from the heat and stir in the beaten egg yolks, lemon juice and grated cheese and serve immediately.

FAGIOLI ALLA PROVINCIALE

Haricot beans

TO SERVE 4

1 pint haricot beans, which have been al- lowed to soak over- night in cold water	1 small onion chopped small
¼ pint tomato sauce (see page 217)	1 teaspoon chopped parsley
	2 oz. butter
	1 clove garlic, crushed

Drain the beans and cook in boiling, salted water for about 1 hour or until tender; drain. Meanwhile, in a stewpan heat the butter and in it brown the chopped onion and garlic, add the drained beans and the parsley, add pepper and salt to taste and the tomato sauce. Cook together for a further 10 minutes.

HARICOT BEANS WITH BACON

TO SERVE 4

12 oz. haricot beans, soaked overnight, and cooked till tender in boiling salted water, using 1 pint water, and cooking for about 1 hour. Do not throw away the water in which they have been cooked but place in a fireproof casserole and add:
1 teaspoon dry mustard

3 tablespoons molasses or black treacle
3 oz. brown sugar
salt to taste
2 tablespoons vinegar
2 tablespoons tomato conserve moistened with 4 tablespoons warm water
4 oz. bacon or ham cut in small squares
1 small onion chopped fine

Cover and cook in a really slow oven (275° F. or Regulo 1 is quite hot enough) for 6 or 8 hours, looking at them from time to time and adding more water if they appear to be becoming too dry.

FAVE AL GUNCIALE

Broad Beans with bacon

TO SERVE 4

2 lb. broad beans, and
if you wish really to
enjoy them, gather
them while they are
still small and tender

2 slices streaky bacon
1 oz. butter
1 medium sized onion

Heat the butter in a stewpan, in it cook the chopped onion until it is a golden yellow colour, add the bacon cut in dice, and when this is cooked, add the shelled uncooked beans, and cook together for a further 5 minutes; add water almost to cover; place lid on stewpan and simmer gently for 20 minutes. Add pepper and salt to taste.

PISELLI AL PROSCIUTTO

Green Peas with Ham

TO SERVE 4

2 lb. peas
1 small onion

4 oz. ham cut in dice
1 oz. butter

Melt the butter in a stewpan, cook the chopped onion till a golden yellow; add the diced ham and cook for a further 5 minutes, then add the peas, shelled, washed but not cooked; add sufficient water not quite to cover, and cook gently for 15 minutes with the lid on the stewpan.

PISELLI ALLA PARIGINA

Peas, Paris style

TO SERVE 4

A French recipe, but one which finds its way into Italian cookery books and on to Italian tables, so well worth including.

2 lb. peas	2 round lettuces
4 spring onions	2 teaspoons castor sugar
salt and pepper	1 oz. butter

Shell the peas, and retain 4 or 5 of the best-looking shells. Wash the lettuces and cut in four lengthways, then lift out of the water and place dripping wet in a stewpan in which you have already warmed the butter, add the peas and the pea pods you have kept aside, the onions and pepper and salt; cover and allow to cook slowly for 45 minutes, shaking the pan from time to time to prevent the vegetables sticking. Take a look from time to time, and if the peas look like becoming dry, add a teaspoon or 2 of warm water. 5 minutes before serving, add the sugar and shake the pan to mix well.

Aubergines

These luscious-looking vegetables make delicious eating cooked in various ways.

MELANZANE RIPIENE

Stuffed aubergines

TO SERVE 4

2 large aubergines	2 slices bread, soaked
1 small onion chopped	in milk and squeezed dry
2 slices of ham diced	4 oz. chopped mush-
1 oz. butter	rooms
4 oz. tomatoes	salt and pepper

Split the aubergines in two lengthways and scoop out the middle of the flesh, and place on one side. Meanwhile, heat the butter in a small pan. In it cook the chopped onion until it is a golden yellow, add the tomatoes, cut small, the chopped mushrooms and the ham, and sauté together for 5 minutes. Add the bread and the flesh of the aubergines cut small and mix well together, adding pepper and salt to taste. Fill the aubergines with the mixture, lay in a fireproof baking dish side by side, dot with butter and bake in a slow oven for about an hour.

MELANZANE ALLA NAPOLITANA
Aubergines Neapolitan style
TO SERVE 4

3 or 4 medium sized aubergines	salt and pepper
4 oz. Bel Paese, unless you are in Italy, in which case use an equal quantity of Mozzarella	2 oz. grated Parmesan
	¾ pint or rather more tomato sauce (see page 217)
	flour
	oil for frying

For this dish peel the aubergines, cut in ½-inch slices cross-ways, sprinkle with salt, cover and leave for an hour or so, then drain, flour lightly and fry gently in hot olive oil, then drain on blotting paper to remove the surplus oil.

Grease or oil a soufflé dish or fireproof casserole and in it put alternate layers of aubergines, Bel Paese cheese and toma-to sauce until all is used up; sprinkle with the grated Parmesan and dot with butter. Bake in a moderate oven for 25 minutes.

MELANZANE ALLA GENOVESE
Aubergines Genoese style
TO SERVE 4

3 or 4 medium sized aubergines	1 tablespoon olive oil
1 chopped onion	2 or 3 ripe tomatoes
salt and pepper	2 eggs

Heat the oil and in it cook the chopped onion until it is golden brown; add the aubergines, cut in ½-inch slices crossways and cook for 5 minutes, then add the tomatoes, peeled and cut in pieces, and cook together until the aubergines are tender; remove from the fire and stir in 2 lightly beaten eggs; mix well and serve immediately.

CIPOLLE RIPIENE
Stuffed onions
TO SERVE 4

For this you need the large Spanish type, allowing 1 onion per person. Cook them in boiling water for 15 minutes, drain, remove the centre and fill with stuffing as suggested for aubergines, adding a few chopped black olives if liked. Place in a fireproof baking dish, dot with butter and bake in a slow oven for an hour.

POTATO PANCAKES
TO SERVE 4

4 large potatoes	2 medium sized onions
2 tablespoons flour	salt and pepper to taste

Grate the raw potatoes, draining off any surplus liquid; add the chopped or grated onion, flour and seasoning, mixing thoroughly. Drop by spoonfuls into very hot oil in a frying pan and cook golden brown.

PATATE IN STUFATO

Sautéed potatoes

TO SERVE 4

4 large potatoes
2 tablespoons butter
1 tablespoon tomato
   conserve

1 slice fat roast beef
1 teaspoon chopped
   rosemary

Heat the butter in a stewpan, add the beef cut in dice and fry till brown. Then add the potatoes peeled and cut in thin slices, and the rosemary, pepper and salt, and finally the tomato conserve thinned with a little water; cook over moderate heat for 45 minutes, stirring now and again and adding a little boiling water if the dish appears to be drying.

POTATO FRITTERS

1 lb. potatoes
2 whole eggs and
   2 extra yolks

2 oz. butter
a few chopped pistachio or pine nuts

Cook the potatoes and mash in a pestle and mortar or pass through a ricer, adding the butter, beaten eggs and chopped nuts. Form into small rissoles, dip in egg white and fry in hot olive oil. Drain and serve very hot.

PATATE ARROSTE

Baked potatoes

TO SERVE 4

Allow 1 good-sized potato per person; peel and place in a baking dish with 1 oz. or more of butter, and bake in a moderate oven for 1 hour or until they are nicely browned but not burnt; baste from time to time with the butter and sprinkle lightly with salt.

PATATE CON SALSA DI POMODORO

Potatoes with tomato sauce

TO SERVE 4

4 large potatoes
1 medium sized onion,
  chopped

½ pint tomato sauce
  (see page 217)
1 tablespoon oil

Heat the oil and in it cook the chopped onion till a golden brown; add the potatoes, peeled and cut in slices, simmer for a few minutes, then add the tomato sauce, together with a little water and cook gently till the potatoes are tender and the liquid has reduced and thickened — about 40 minutes.

PATATE AL BURRO

Buttered potatoes

TO SERVE 4

4 large potatoes
1 tablespoon chopped
  parsley

3 tablespoons stock
2 oz. butter

Peel the potatoes and cut in slices, and place in a stewpan with the stock and the parsley and cook over moderate heat until the potatoes are cooked, adding a little water from time to time if they appear to be drying up; 5 minutes before serving add the butter. Mix well together and serve hot.

TOMATOES COOKED WITH ONIONS

TO SERVE 4

1 large tin tomatoes
salt and pepper
1 tablespoon castor
  sugar

1 oz. butter
3 medium sized onions
1 cup breadcrumbs

Drain the tomatoes, saving the liquid to add to the stock pot. Sprinkle the tomatoes with salt, pepper and sugar. Peel and slice the onions, and in a buttered fireproof dish arrange alternate layers of tomatoes, onions and breadcrumbs, finishing with a layer of breadcrumbs. Dot with butter and bake in a moderate oven for 30 minutes.

POMODORI ALLA CASALINGA

Tomatoes, housewife style

TO SERVE 4

1 lb. firm tomatoes
pinch oregano
salt and pepper
1 tablespoon olive oil

1 clove garlic, crushed
1 tablespoon chopped
  parsley
1 tablespoon grated
  Parmesan

Halve the tomatoes, removing the seeds; place in a greased fireproof dish, sprinkling with a mixture of salt, pepper, oregano, garlic and parsley, and finally with the grated cheese and oil; bake in moderate oven for 20 minutes.

CANDIED CARROTS

Peel carrots and cut in dice; cook in boiling, salted water for 10 minutes; drain. Heat a little butter in a heavy pan, add the carrots, and over them sprinkle a little brown sugar. Cook slowly, stirring from time to time to prevent sticking, until the carrots are glazed and tender. A little Marsala is a welcome addition, but if this is used, allow to evaporate, so that in the finished dish you have the carrots glazed, tender, but not liquid.

CARROTS COOKED IN BUTTER

For this you need carrots that are not too tiny. Peel the carrots and cut in lengthways strips, cook for 10 minutes in boiling, salted water, then drain, and place in a stewpan with a good knob of butter, pepper and salt. Allow them to cook gently in the butter for 10 minutes, then add 2 or 3 tablespoons of meat stock that has been thickened with a little flour. At the end of another 10 minutes, during which you have stirred the pan to prevent the carrots sticking, add a little cayenne pepper and sprinkle with the juice of $\frac{1}{2}$ lemon before serving.

CAROTE AL BURRO
Buttered carrots

TO SERVE 4

1 lb. young carrots, washed, scraped and cut in slices	pinch cinnamon
	salt and pepper
1 oz. butter	1 tablespoon flour
3 tablespoons stock	juice of $\frac{1}{2}$ lemon

Boil the carrots in salted water for 15 minutes, drain, and place in a buttered fireproof dish with the butter, pepper and salt, stir in the flour and gently add the stock, and allow to cook in a moderate oven or on top of the stove for 10 minutes; finally, 5 minutes before serving, add the cinnamon and lemon juice.

BROCCOLI STRASCICATI
Broccoli with salt pork

Prepare the broccoli and cook in boiling salted water for 15 minutes; drain. Place in a stewpan with a little salt pork cut in dice and cook over a very slow fire for 30 minutes until the fat has been absorbed by the broccoli. No further salting will be necessary, as there will be sufficient salt in the pork.

BRUSSELS SPROUTS SERVED WITH CHESTNUTS
TO SERVE 4

2 lb. good, hard Brussels sprouts	8 oz. chestnuts
1 tablespoon brown sugar	3 oz. butter
	1 tablespoon flour
	salt

Cook the sprouts in boiling salted water, and when draining them save about ½ pint of the water in which they have been cooked. Meanwhile, blanch and peel the chestnuts and boil in salted water until tender — about 25 minutes. Heat the butter in a small stewpan and in it brown the flour; stir in the sugar and mix well, then slowly add the ½ pint of water from the sprouts, and stir until the mixture thickens. Mix the chestnuts and sprouts together, cover with this sauce, and place in a warm oven until heated through.

CAVOLFIORE ALLA LIONESE

Cauliflower with meat sauce

TO SERVE 4

1 good-sized cauliflower	½ pint meat sauce (see page 230)

Cook the cauliflower for 10 minutes only in boiling salted water, then drain and place in cold water for a few minutes; drain again and break into small pieces, and place in a stewpan with the meat sauce and allow to cook a further 20 minutes over moderate heat, adding a little stock or water if it appears to be getting too dry.

CAVOLFIORE ALLA SICILIANA

Cauliflower Sicilian style

TO SERVE 4

1 cauliflower	3 tablespoons tomato
2 anchovies	sauce (see page 217)
oil	1 teaspoon capers

Cook cauliflower for 15 minutes in boiling, slightly salted water, drain and place in greased fireproof dish. Sprinkle over top the chopped anchovies and bake in moderate oven for 15 minutes, basting with a little oil from time to time. Finally add tomato sauce and capers and allow to cook a few minutes longer before serving in the dish in which it was cooked.

PURÉE OF CHESTNUTS

TO SERVE 6

1 lb. of chestnuts from which outer and inner skins have been removed	a little warm milk salt and pepper 1 oz. butter

Boil the chestnuts in salted water until tender, then drain, and mash with just enough warm milk to moisten them; add butter and pepper and salt to taste. Serve instead of mashed potatoes.

MARROWS OR ZUCCHINI

Whenever I am faced with a helping of boiled marrow, served in the English fashion, with white sauce, I think fondly of the more enterprising Italian ways of dealing with this vegetable.

In the fruit and vegetable shops during the summer the tiny imported *zucchini* (or *courgettes*) are to be seen, and may be bought at luxury prices, but there is no reason why English marrows should not be harvested while they are still young and tender and used in recipes for which *zucchini* have been prescribed. Take for example some of the following:

ZUCCHINE FRITTI

Fried small marrows

TO SERVE 4

You need either 1 lb. zucchine, or a small English marrow of equal weight. Cut into rounds about $\frac{3}{8}$ inch thick, spread on a plate, and cover with a sprinkling of salt. Place an inverted plate over them and leave for an hour, by the end of which time the liquid will have come out of them. Drain thoroughly, then flour them and fry them in hot olive oil, allowing about a minute for each side. Drain them well before serving, so as to remove surplus oil, and serve with sections of lemon.

STEWED SMALL MARROWS

TO SERVE 4

1 lb. small marrows	3 good-sized onions
3 tablespoons olive oil	¼ pint water
	salt and pepper to taste

Heat the oil and in it cook the chopped onion until it is golden brown. Add the marrows, unpeeled if you have the actual zucchine. If you are using English marrows, these too may be unpeeled provided they are quite small, but if you are using the larger variety, then peel and cut into 1-inch slices. Add water and seasoning; cover the pan and cook slowly for 30 minutes.

MARROW WITH TOMATO

As a variation of the above dish, omit the water and add instead of it either 2 large tomatoes peeled and sliced, or a small tin of tomatoes, and, if procurable, a teaspoon of chopped basil, or failing this, a similar amount of chopped parsley. Keep an eye on the dish while cooking, and if it looks as though it is drying out, add a very little water from time to time.

STUFFED MARROW

TO SERVE 4

1 lb. small marrows	salt, pepper and
chopped ham	pinch rosemary mixed
breadcrumbs	well together

Split the marrows in two lengthways, and remove the seeds. Fill the hollows with the stuffing, put the two halves of the marrows together again and tie with white cotton to keep the stuffing in. Heat a little butter in a stewpan, add the marrows, brown them lightly, then reduce the heat and cover the pan, and cook for a further 20 minutes.

SPINACH

Remember the necessity of washing spinach thoroughly; 7 waters were at one time prescribed, and unless the spinach is phenomenally free from grit and sand, 7 waters will not prove to be too many. To cook so as to retain as much as possible of the natural flavour, do not place the spinach in water, but after the last washing, lift it from the vessel with the hands, shake it well and place it in a saucepan large enough to hold the mass, without the addition of further water; sprinkle with salt and cook over a low heat for 10 or 15 minutes, pressing it down from time to time with a fork to ensure even cooking.

SPINACH AS SERVED IN ROME

TO SERVE 4

Having prepared and cooked 1 lb. spinach as directed above for 10 minutes, add to it 3 tablespoons good olive oil, and pepper and salt to taste. Mix well and serve very hot.

SPINACI ALLA PARMIGIANA

Spinach with Parmesan cheese

TO SERVE 4

1 lb. spinach	butter
salt, pepper and nutmeg	2 tablespoons grated Parmesan

Cook the spinach as directed above, and when cooked drain well, then place in a stewpan with about 2 oz. butter, salt, pepper and a pinch of nutmeg. Allow the butter to melt, then stir in the grated cheese and serve hot.

SPINACI ALLA PIEMONTESE

TO SERVE 4

1 lb. spinach	6 or 8 anchovies cut
1 oz. butter or 1 table-	small
spoon olive oil	½ clove garlic,
salt and pepper to taste	crushed

Cook the spinach as directed and drain well. Heat the butter
in a pan, add the garlic and cook till yellow, add the spinach,
anchovies and pepper and salt to taste, mix well together,
and serve decorated with triangles of thin toast.

Salads

The salad most commonly met with in Italy is the fresh green salad, liberally doused with good olive oil and lemon juice, but there are a fair number of other salads to be met with when one spends a longer time in the country, and here are a few suggestions.

ONION SALAD

Allow 1 large or 2 medium sized onions per person.

Either bake the onions in the oven, or boil them until they are cooked but not mushy. Allow to cool and when cold, slice them fairly thinly, spread in layers on a flat dish and season with olive oil, lemon juice and pepper and salt.

MIXED SALAD

Slice thinly a few gherkins, and a green pepper, add some cooked meat — ham, veal, pork or chicken for preference — cut in small pieces, a few cold boiled new potatoes, and if liked 1 or 2 anchovies, boned and cut small. Mix well together and serve with an oil and vinegar dressing.

MIXED SALAD WITH HARD-BOILED EGG

Take 3 or 4 cold boiled potatoes (not floury ones), a beetroot cooked in the oven and cooled. Cut the vegetables into dice, and to them add 2 small gherkins, cut in thin slices. Combine these with a head of endive, washed carefully and torn into pieces. Mix well, and toss in an oil and vinegar dressing; sprinkle with capers, and decorate with 3 or 4 anchovies, and one hard-boiled egg per person, peeled and cut in two lengthways.

INSALATA ALLA GIARDINIERA
Gardener's wife's salad

Mix together any left-over cooked young vegetables, small young potatoes, peas, beans, etc., together with peeled, sliced tomatoes, and serve with a dressing of oil and vinegar, pepper and salt.

PLAIN SALAD

Cos or Batavian lettuce, washed well and hung in a salad drainer until crisp, is excellent by itself served with a plain oil and vinegar dressing, mixed well. (See *Dressing for green salad*, page 227.)

SALAD WITH HARD-BOILED EGG

Allow 1 hard-boiled egg per person, cut in two lengthways and arrange on top of a bed of lettuce dressed as previously suggested with an oil and vinegar dressing; or if liked, serve individual plates of dressed lettuce, with egg cut lengthways decorating each portion.

With all green salads, remember not to add the dressing until the last possible moment before serving, and remember, too, that torn lettuce is preferable to lettuce cut with knife or scissors.

CUCUMBER SALAD

Slice thinly an unpeeled cucumber; spread the slices on a flat plate, sprinkle with salt, cover with another plate and leave for about 2 hours. Drain, and squeeze moisture out of the slices by placing in a cloth and squeezing in the hands. Season with oil, wine vinegar (or lemon juice), pepper and salt to taste, and, for additional enjoyment, a little castor sugar.

SALAD WITH SOUR CREAM

When eggs are plentiful, hard-boil half a dozen, and having passed the yolks through a sieve, mix with 1 gill or thereabouts of sour cream; add a pinch of salt, freshly ground black pepper and 2 teaspoons or a little more of wine vinegar, and use as a salad dressing on a mixture of lettuce and sliced fresh cucumber.

Sweets

Sweets met with on vacation in Italy seem to be of two kinds; either the welcome, well-filled dish of fruits in season, or the outsize very rich, very creamy 'layer cake', but a longer stay discloses other, more imaginative sweets, and a selection of these is given in the following pages.

ZABAGLIONE or ZABAIONE

When talking of sweets in the Italian menu, this airy-fairy refinement of egg punch is the one that springs first to the mind, and it is worth while knowing how to make it to perfection.

For each consumer allow 2 egg yolks, 2 tablespoons castor sugar, and 2 tablespoons of Marsala, or failing this, of good sherry. Vanilla may be added, if liked, but for my taste the dish is better without it.

Beat together the egg yolks and sugar until they are pale and creamy, then slowly add the Marsala. Place the mixture over hot water in a double boiler, and stir slowly until it thickens, taking care not to overcook it, otherwise it will curdle. Serve immediately in warmed sherbet glasses. There is a school of thought that dictates 'serve hot or cold', but this to most Italian palates is heresy — serve your zabaione hot.

CREMA DI BAGNOMARIA

Rich steamed custard

TO SERVE 4

2 eggs, plus 4 extra egg yolks	3 tablespoons castor sugar
½ pint milk	grated rind of ½ lemon
butter for greasing dish	— alternatively, ½ teaspoon vanilla essence

Grate the lemon rind into the milk, or alternatively add the vanilla, and allow it to stand for 30 minutes. Break the eggs and extra yolks into a basin, and beat together with the sugar, then add the milk gradually. When thoroughly mixed, pass through a fine sieve, removing all the froth that has formed in the beating. Place the liquid in a greased soufflé dish and place this in a double boiler, or if one is not available, place it on an inverted sandwich cake tin, in a saucepan of boiling water, with the water reaching to within 1½ inches from the top of the outside of the soufflé dish. Cook on top of the stove, keeping the water just under boiling point for about an hour. If you propose eating this dish hot, allow to stand for about

10 minutes after it has finished cooking, before serving. Alternatively it may be allowed to become cold, when it makes a delicious cold sweet.

Fritters

Starting off with a frying batter as a basis, delicious fritters may be made of the various fruits as they come into season.

STANDARD FRYING BATTER

4 oz. plain flour
¼ pint or rather more
  of warm water

3 tablespoons olive oil
a pinch of salt
1 lightly beaten egg white

Sieve the flour into a basin, make a well in the centre and into this pour the oil; mix well, and add the salt, then slowly add the water, stirring constantly until the consistency of thick cream is obtained. Allow to stand for 2 hours or thereabouts, then stir in the lightly beaten egg white, and use as a coating for fish or for fruits as suggested in the following pages.

APPLE FRITTERS

For these use Bramleys or similar large cooking apples, allowing one per person. Peel the apples, and remove the core with a metal corer, then slice the apples transversely in slices about ⅜ inch in thickness, dip in batter, and fry in hot oil; drain, sprinkle with castor sugar and serve very hot.

An improvement is to substitute for half the water of the batter an equal amount of white wine.

A refinement of these fritters also is to be obtained by immersing the apples, once they are peeled and cored, but before slicing them, in rum to which sugar and a pinch of cinnamon have been added, allowing them to remain for 2 or 3 hours, turning them frequently so as to impregnate the fruit with the rum, but in this case, the water batter is sufficiently rich without the addition of white wine.

PEAR FRITTERS

Using the same method, but instead of slicing the fruit, peel them, quarter them and core them before dipping in batter. Hard cooking pears make delicious fritters.

PEACH FRITTERS

Peel the peaches, halve them and remove the stone. Immerse for several hours in white wine to which sugar has been added; remove, drain, dip in frying batter and fry in hot olive oil.

FIG FRITTERS

For these you need fresh figs that are not over-ripe. Cut the fruit in two lengthways, and spread on a plate, sprinkling them with sugar and with a few drops of a good liqueur, Benedictine, Rosolio, or some similar liqueur. Leave for 2 or 3 hours, then drain, sprinkle lightly with flour, dip in frying batter, and fry in hot oil; drain and serve hot, sprinkled with castor sugar.

PLUM FRITTERS

Again use fruit that is not over-ripe. Place in a warm oven for 30 minutes, then cut in halves, remove the stones, and spread on a dish, sprinkling with sugar and a few drops of rum and a pinch of cinnamon. Leave for 2 or 3 hours, then drain, dip in frying batter and fry as directed for the previous fruit fritters.

CHESTNUT FRITTERS

To 8 oz. chestnut flour, add sufficient water to make a thick paste; add a pinch of salt, a few seedless raisins, and a few chopped pistachio nuts; mix together well and drop in spoonfuls into deep hot oil, cooking till golden brown. Drain and serve hot, sprinkled with castor sugar.

APRICOT FRITTERS

For these the apricots should not be over-ripe. Cut in two, removing the stones; place in a vessel deep enough to hold them when sprinkled with sugar; leave for several hours, or even for a whole day, then remove and drain, dip in frying batter and fry in hot oil, drain and serve hot, sprinkled with castor sugar.

Alternatively, instead of covering with sugar and leaving for some hours, the apricots may be covered with rum, to which has been added sugar and a pinch of cinnamon, left for 2 or 3 hours, then drained, dipped in batter and fried.

SEMOLINA FRITTERS

1 pint milk	4 tablespoons sugar
pinch salt	4 oz. semolina
egg yolks	2 egg whites
a little candied citron	2 oz. raisins

Heat the milk with the sugar and salt and when it begins to boil, place in the top of a double boiler, and add the semolina little by little until a thick paste is formed, stirring continually so that it does not stick to the bottom of the saucepan; remove from the heat, cool slightly and add the beaten egg yolks and later the whites beaten stiffly, the citron cut small and the raisins. Mix together well, and when cool, form into little balls the size of a walnut; dip in beaten egg white and then in breadcrumbs and fry quickly in deep oil until a golden brown; drain for a moment or two on blotting paper to drain off any surplus oil, and serve hot, sprinkled liberally with castor sugar.

FRITTELLE ALLA FIORENTINA

To 8 oz. fine flour add sufficient water to make a thick paste; add a pinch of salt, the yolk of an egg, a little grated lemon rind and a few seedless raisins. Mix well and drop in spoonfuls into deep hot oil and fry until golden brown. Drain and serve hot.

SWEET FRITTERS

2 egg yolks	2 oz. flour
1 pint cream	a little finely chopped
2 tablespoons sugar	candied citron

Beat together the egg yolks, cream and sugar until well mixed, blend in the flour and place in a double boiler, cooking till thick and being careful not to allow it to boil, otherwise the egg yolks will curdle. If the cream does not seem to be thick enough, a little semolina may be added towards the end of the cooking time. Stir in the citron.

Pour on to a flat plate that has been lightly oiled or greased with butter; allow to cool, cut in pieces about 2 inches square; dip in white of egg and then in breadcrumbs, fry in butter till golden brown. Serve hot, sprinkled with sugar.

MONT BLANC
TO SERVE 4

1 lb. Italian chestnuts	8 oz. castor sugar
¼ pint double cream	salt

Cut a slit in the chestnuts at the pointed end, and place them a dozen at a time in a very hot oven for 10 minutes, after which they will peel easily. When all are peeled, place in boiling water and allow to simmer for an hour or until they are tender. Strain, and mash the nuts, adding the sugar and a pinch of salt. Pass them then through a potato ricer, allowing them to pile up in pyramid form on a dish. The less you touch them with your hands the better, otherwise the light appearance of the finished dish is apt to be spoiled.

Whip the cream, flavouring it if you like with a little good liqueur, and pile it lightly on the top of the mound of chestnuts, rather like snow on a mountain top.

CHARLOTTE DI MELE, PERE O PESCHE

Apple, pear or peach charlotte

TO SERVE 4

2 lb. cooking apples, pears or peaches that are not over-ripe
grated rind of 1 lemon
1½ tablespoons rum
4 oz. brown sugar
1 tablespoon cold water
1 oz. butter
1½ tablespoons white wine
thin slices of bread and butter with crusts removed

Prepare the fruit by peeling and coring (or in the case of peaches, removing the stones), put them in a stewpan with the sugar, the water and the white wine and cook until tender; when the fruit is reduced to a pulp, add the butter and the grated lemon rind, and if not sufficiently sweet add a little more sugar. Meanwhile, grease a soufflé mould, and line it entirely with well-buttered slices of thin bread. Pour in the fruit pulp, and over the top place a layer of thinly sliced and buttered bread. Sprinkle with sugar. Bake in a moderate oven for 30 minutes and just before serving, pour over the rum and light, so that the dish is carried flaming to the table. This final touch may be omitted if preferred.

BODINO DI LATTE ALLA MANDORLE
Milk pudding with almonds
TO SERVE 4

For those who like almonds, here is a refinement of milk
pudding that is worthy of attention.

1 pint milk	butter for greasing
2 oz. almonds	a soufflé dish
2 slices of bread with	4 to 5 oz. castor sugar,
crust removed, soaked	depending on personal
in milk and squeezed	taste
dry	6 whole eggs and two
	extra yolks

Blanch the almonds in boiling water and remove the skins,
then in a mortar pound them to a paste, uniting them with the
soaked and squeezed bread. Meanwhile heat the milk in
a double boiler, with the sugar added; when the milk reaches
boiling point, add the paste of almonds and bread, little by
little, and cook a few minutes longer, stirring so that it does
not stick to the bottom of the pan. Remove from the fire
and slowly add the beaten eggs and extra yolks, mixing well.
Meanwhile, grease your soufflé dish, and pour in the milk
mixture, and cook for 1 hour in an oven that is not too
fierce (the heat you use for rice pudding should be right for
this). Serve hot, and if you wish to make it even more luxurious,
prepare a zabaglione, and serve at the same time.

BODINO DI GABINETTO
Cabinet pudding
TO SERVE 4

stale Savoy fingers
4 oz. ratafia biscuits
2 whole eggs and 2 extra
   yolks
grated rind of $\frac{1}{2}$ lemon

$\frac{3}{4}$ pint milk
1 tablespoon castor sugar
a tablespoon each of
   sultanas and of chop-
   ped citron
a few glacé cherries and
   a little shredded angelica

Grease a 1½-pint soufflé dish with butter, and line the sides
with stale Savoy biscuits — or failing these, stale sponge cakes
cut in thin slices lengthways; arrange at the bottom of the
mould a layer of the sultanas, mixed with the chopped
citron, cherries and angelica, and on this place the ratafias
broken small and any trimmings left over from the Savoy
biscuits or sponge cakes.

Beat together the eggs, extra yolks and sugar, and when the
sugar is dissolved, beat in the milk and grated rind slowly,
and strain into the mould.

You may now either cover with buttered paper and steam
gently for an hour, or place in a not too fierce oven and bake
for a similar length of time.

Serve with whipped cream, or with a little apricot jam
warmed.

CROSTINI ALL'ANANASSO
Pineapple toast

This is a dish worth trying when fresh pineapples are available at reasonable prices.

1 or 2 small pineapples	12 thin slices of bread
4 oz. butter	with the crusts re-
a few teaspoons of ma-	moved, and cut in
raschino or kirsch	two lengthways
4 oz. sugar	a little apricot jam
	2 tablespoons water

Heat the butter in a heavy pan and in it fry the bread very lightly, not so much browning it as allowing it to absorb the butter. Previously, peel the pineapples and cut into as many slices as there are pieces of bread, lay these on a plate, sprinkle lightly with sugar and with the liqueur and allow it to stay for 2 or 3 hours. When the pineapple has 'marinated' and the bread is cooked, arrange in a flat fireproof dish, with a piece of pineapple on each piece of bread.

Cook the sugar with the water until it begins to colour, and to this add the liquid in which the pineapple has marinated, together with the apricot jam; boil together for a few minutes, then pass through a sieve and serve boiling hot over the *crostini*.

MERINGUES

Since so many of the foregoing recipes call for extra egg yolks a recipe for meringues is useful for employing the whites left over.

Light the oven before starting to make the meringues, and it should be a very slow oven (250° F. or Regulo ½ at most).

4 egg whites	8 oz. castor sugar
a pinch of salt	½ teaspoon vanilla, if liked

Beat the egg whites with a beater, together with the pinch of salt, until they are stiff and dry; now add half the sugar a little at a time, beating thoroughly after each addition; beat in the vanilla; the balance of the sugar should be folded in with a spatula or fork.

Meanwhile run some sheets of brown paper under the cold water tap and use as linings for flat 'cookie' tins. Drop the egg mixture by large spoonfuls on to the paper, place them in the oven and allow to cook for 45 to 60 minutes, or until they will lift easily from the paper. The slow cooking is essential, the trick being to dry out the mixture rather than to cook it.

When cooled, serve filled with ice cream, whipped cream, or any sweetened fruit.

PASTICCIO DI FRUTTA

Fruit flan

Prepare 2 lb. mixed fruit in season, apples, apricots, plums, pears, etc. and place to cook in a stewpan with 4 oz. granulated sugar and 1 gill white wine. A few soaked and stoned prunes make a welcome addition to the mixture. When the fruit is tender, add a little chopped candied citron, 2 tablespoons of rum and a pinch of powdered cinnamon.

Meanwhile line flan tins with fairly rich pastry; pour in the fruit and bake in a hot oven until the pastry is cooked.

Serve hot or cold, with whipped cream.

SFOGLIATE DOLCE DI RICOTTA

Sfogliate are little *bonnes-bouches* of the lightest of light puff paste, filled with various fillings; a good number are filled, as are our vol-au-vents, with minced chicken, shrimps and other savoury fillings; here is one in which ricotta cheese is suggested, but which can be made here with the substitution of cream cheese for the unobtainable ricotta.

Prepare a supply of puff pastry made of equal quantities (say 4 oz. each) of flour and butter.

For the filling:

8 oz. cream cheese
1 tablespoon sultanas
1 teaspoon rum
4 oz. castor sugar

1 tablespoon candied
  orange peel
a few drops of vanilla

For the cream:

1 egg yolk
1 oz. flour

½ tablespoon sugar
1½ tablespoons milk

Beat egg and sugar for coating the sfogliate before baking. 30 minutes before starting to cook, place the chopped orange peel and the sultanas in a cup with the rum, and allow them to absorb it before adding them to the mixture of cream cheese and sugar.

Combine the egg yolk, sugar and flour, gently add the milk and cook together in a double boiler till it has thickened; mix with the cheese mixture.

Divide the puff pastry into squares about 3 inches on each side; brush with beaten egg; in the centre of each place a teaspoon of the filling, and fold the pastry over cornerways, pressing the edges together; brush the top with beaten egg, and bake in a hot oven for 20 minutes; 5 minutes before finishing cooking, remove from the oven and sprinkle liberally with castor sugar, which will caramelise slightly, when the sfogliate are returned to the heat.

PIZZA ALLA CAMPOFRANCO

TO SERVE 8

8 oz. plain flour
5 eggs
½ tablespoon sugar
4 oz. ham
3 tablespoons grated
  Parmesan
5 oz. butter

1 teaspoon chopped
  basil
½ oz. brewers' yeast
8 oz. Bel Paese cheese
1 lb. tomatoes
1 tablespoon olive oil
salt and pepper

Pile the flour on to your pastry board or cooking table, make a hollow in it and in this put the butter, 2 eggs, a pinch of salt and the yeast diluted with a little water or milk. Work the flour with the hands until the ingredients are absorbed, then blend in the next 2 eggs, and work the dough until it is elastic to the touch; then add the sugar; work the dough a little more; then place in a warmed basin. Cover with a cloth and leave in a fairly warm place for 2 hours, by which time it should have doubled in size.

Meanwhile prepare the filling; slice the cheese, and the ham; peel the tomatoes and remove the seeds, and cook very quickly in oil so that they do not become mushy but retain their firmness.

When the dough has risen, flour your pastry board; divide the dough in 2 pieces, one slightly larger than the other and roll out into 2 circles. With the larger one, line a greased pie plate or flan tin, and on it lay first of all a layer of the cheese, then a layer of the cooked tomatoes. Season with salt and pepper and a little basil, and on this place a layer of strips of ham; continue in this way till the filling is all used up, and finish off with a layer of the grated Parmesan. Now beat the fifth egg, and with a brush paint the edges of the dough, and over it place the smaller circle of dough, pressing the edges together so that they remain closed; leave it to rise again in a warm place, for about an hour, then paint the top with the balance of the beaten egg, and cook for 20 to 25 minutes in a hot oven. Eat hot.

PIZZA

A book of Italian cookery would be incomplete without a recipe for this Neapolitan speciality — try it if you like; speaking for myself, the mention of pizza will always recall what arrived at my table in Naples one evening when, fancying 'something not too heavy', I ordered pizza. I waited a few moments and was then confronted with an outsize dinner plate, on which reposed something that looked rather like King Henry the Eighth's best hat made of pastry that was solid rather than light, and filled with a mixture of tomatoes and anchovies that, to say the least, was rich, and alarmingly salty. However, if it's pizza you fancy, here's how it is made.

Sauces

The preparation of a sauce is a ritual in Italy; it is not unusual for an Italian housewife to spend hours in loving preparation of a truly rich and enjoyable sauce to be eaten over *pasta*, and having tasted the results of some of the hours of loving labour, one has to admit the time has been well spent.

BÉCHAMEL SAUCE

| 1½ oz. butter | 2 tablespoons flour |
| 1 pint heated milk | salt and pepper |

Allow butter to melt in saucepan, but before it turns brown lower heat, and blend in flour, stirring until smooth; then little by little add heated milk, stirring constantly. If liked add a pinch of nutmeg when adding the seasonings, or alternatively allow a bay leaf to remain in the sauce during its final cooking, which should be 15 minutes from the time the milk, flour and butter are blended together. It is a good idea to use the top of a double boiler for making this sauce, placing it over the boiling water in the lower part of the boiler for the last 15 minutes of cooking time. If it is too thick, add a little more milk from time to time.

If you have used a bay leaf for flavouring, remove before serving.

If the sauce is made well in advance, cover with a lid to prevent a skin forming.

VARIATIONS OF BÉCHAMEL SAUCE

Cheese Sauce

Make sauce as directed for plain béchamel sauce, and when cooked, add 6 to 8 tablespoons grated Parmesan cheese and blend well before serving.

Excellent over cooked broccoli or cauliflower.

Egg and Parsley Sauce

To 1 pint of béchamel sauce made as directed, allow 2 hard-boiled eggs and 3 tablespoons finely chopped fresh parsley; stir in just before serving. A variation is to add also 1 teaspoon finely chopped mint.

Excellent with broccoli, cauliflower or fish dishes.

Mushroom Sauce

While your béchamel sauce is cooking, wash and chop finely 4 oz. mushrooms and cook gently for 10 minutes in hot olive oil before adding to the béchamel.

Shrimp Sauce

To a pint of béchamel sauce add a ½ pint of shrimps, shelled and chopped, and serve when heated through.
A good sauce with fish.

BROWN SAUCE

1 small onion chopped finely
2 tablespoons chopped parsley
1 pint beef stock
4 tablespoons flour
1 bay leaf
3 tablespoons olive oil
freshly ground black pepper
1 teaspoon oregano, or, failing this, ¼ teaspoon thyme

Heat oil in heavy pan, brown onion in this with parsley, and stir in flour. When brown and blended add slowly your beef stock; allow to boil for 2 or 3 minutes, and add seasonings.

VARIATIONS OF BROWN SAUCE

Mushroom Sauce

To a ½ pint of brown sauce made as above, add 4 oz. mushrooms that have been washed, chopped finely and cooked for 5 minutes in hot olive oil. Delicious with steak and baked meats.

White Wine Sauce

To ½ pint brown sauce add ¼ pint white wine; heat together to boiling point and serve immediately. A good sauce with baked meat.

PARSLEY BUTTER

1 tablespoon butter
1 teaspoon lemon juice

1 tablespoon finely
  minced parsley
pinch salt

Steak is greatly enhanced with little dabs of this simple sauce.
  Cream butter and blend in remaining ingredients, mixing well and allowing to become very cold before serving at table with steak.

Variations of Parsley Butter

Instead of plain parsley, try the combination of 1 teaspoon each mint, parsley and sweet basil, chopped finely, or, alternatively, 2 teaspoons parsley to 1 teaspoon mint, or 2 teaspoons parsley to 1 teaspoon basil.

ALMOND SAUCE

2 tablespoons butter
juice of 2 lemons

2 oz. blanched chopped
  almonds

Brown butter slightly, and slowly add chopped almonds and lemon juice. Serve hot or cold with fish.

'SOFFRITTO' OR 'BATTUTO'

This is the name given to the foundation from which stews and soups are often started. In its simplest form it consists of hot oil, butter or dripping, in which has been browned a chopped onion or a clove of garlic crushed. It can be elaborated by the addition of chopped carrot, parsley and celery, all very finely chopped and browned before the addition of the meat or game which is to form the stew or soup.

SIMPLE TOMATO SAUCE

1 medium size tin tomatoes
2 onions, chopped finely
1 teaspoon finely chopped basil, or if not available, finely chopped parsley

4 tablespoons olive oil
$\frac{1}{2}$ teaspoon granulated sugar
salt and freshly ground black pepper to taste

Heat oil in a heavy pan, fry onion until transparent and pale yellow, add parsley or basil. Strain tomatoes and add. Cook for 45 minutes, stirring frequently, add sugar and seasonings, and cook gently for a further 10 minutes.

A good sauce to be used with rice or spaghetti.

UNSWEETENED TOMATO SAUCE

This sauce, which uses the tomato purée instead of the tinned tomatoes, needs slightly longer cooking to ensure that the too sharp flavour of the concentrated purée is somewhat diluted.

2 tablespoons tomato
purée
1 clove garlic, crushed
½ teaspoon oregano, or
failing this, ¼ teaspoon
thyme

3 tablespoons olive oil
2 good-sized onions,
sliced
1 pint water
salt and pepper to taste

Heat oil and in it fry onion gently, until transparent and yellow-coloured; add purée, and cook together 2 or 3 minutes, stirring constantly. Add seasonings and water, cover and cook slowly for 1 hour or slightly more, stirring from time to time and adding more water if it becomes too thick. Serve very hot.

TOMATO SAUCE ALLA NAPOLITANA
SUFFICIENT FOR SPAGHETTI FOR 4

1 lb. tomatoes
2 stalks celery
a few leaves of fresh basil

1 onion
1 carrot
salt and pepper to taste

Wash tomatoes, cut in pieces and place in saucepan with other vegetables cut coarsely. Allow to cook slowly for 30 minutes or until the vegetables are tender. Remove from fire and pass through a sieve. Season with pepper and salt. Usually in Naples a knob of fresh lard is added at the end of the cooking and mixed well with the sauce, and just before serving a little freshly chopped basil makes an excellent finishing touch.

TOMATO SAUCE — TO ENRICH

Try the addition of a slice of ham, finely chopped, and/or a glass of Marsala to the finished sauce.

218

WHITE WINE SAUCE TO SERVE WITH FISH

6 tablespoons liquor in which
fish has cooked
2 tablespoons cream
2 tablespoons white wine

1½ oz. butter creamed
and made into a paste
with 1 tablespoon flour
1 oz. extra butter

Place liquor and wine in a saucepan and bring to the boil; add flour and butter paste slowly, and allow to cook for 5 minutes, by the end of which time the sauce will have thickened. Add cream, stirring all the while. Remove from heat and stir in extra 1 oz. butter a little at a time, meanwhile beating the sauce with an egg whisk.

SALSA OLANDESE

Hollandaise Sauce

juice of ½ lemon
4 oz. butter
dash cayenne

2 unbeaten egg yolks
¼ teaspoon salt

An excellent sauce to serve with artichokes or asparagus.

Add lemon juice to unbeaten egg yolks. Divide butter into 3 and add ⅓ also to egg yolks. Cook over hot, but not boiling, water, stirring constantly with a wooden spoon until the butter has melted and the sauce has thickened. Add the second ⅓ of the butter and continue stirring until it has melted and the sauce has thickened again; repeat the process with the remaining ⅓ of the butter, and continue stirring until the sauce has the consistency of mayonnaise. Add the seasonings and beat sauce with a wire whip until it takes on a shiny appearance — about 30 seconds' beating will be needed. It should not curdle, but if it should, beat in a little boiling water until it is smooth.

PIQUANT SAUCE

just under ¼ pint wine
vinegar
6 tablespoons cold water
black pepper
1 teaspoon meat extract
½ teaspoon tomato
paste
½ oz. butter

1 teaspoon flour
½ teaspoon French
mustard
a few finely chopped
capers
1 tablespoon finely
chopped parsley
pinch cayenne pepper

Place vinegar in a saucepan together with a fairly generous
shaking of freshly ground black pepper, and a pinch of
cayenne. Bring to boil and allow to cook until the vinegar
is reduced by half. Add cold water in which you have dissolved
the meat extract and the tomato paste (do not overload the
sauce with tomato paste, keep the quantity small) and allow
to cook together for 10 or 12 minutes; strain through a fine
sieve; replace on stove and re-heat. Cream the butter, and
to it add the flour and when the sauce has reached the boil,
reduce heat and add the butter and flour paste little by little,
stirring with a wooden spoon until the sauce thickens. Cook
slowly for 5 minutes longer, then remove from the fire and
add chopped capers, chopped parsley and mustard.

Excellent with game, pigeons, etc.

TUNNY FISH SAUCE

FOR 1 LB. SPAGHETTI

1 6-oz. tin tunny fish
1 tablespoon chopped
   parsley
1 tablespoon chopped
   capers
salt and pepper

1 lb. (or 1 medium
   sized tin) tomatoes
3 anchovies
3 tablespoons olive oil
1 clove garlic crushed

Heat the oil and in it allow the capers and crushed garlic to cook a few minutes, but do not brown; add tomatoes (cut up, skinned and seeded if raw — strained through a sieve if tinned), and cook for a further 30 minutes. Flake tunny fish small, and chop anchovies finely and add with parsley to the tomato sauce, together with salt and pepper. Cook uncovered until it has become thick.

CLAM SAUCE

Substituting a medium sized tin of clams (drained) for the tunny fish and anchovies of the preceding recipe, you have a favourite sauce for spaghetti frequently met with in and around Naples, except that there the clams come direct out of the sea and not out of tins.

SHRIMP SAUCE

1 pint (before shelling)
   shrimps or prawns
1 tablespoon chopped
   parsley

2 tablespoons olive oil
1 small onion

Chop onion and cook without browning in the heated oil, adding chopped parsley and shelled shrimps, together with warm water to cover, and simmer 20 minutes. The addition of a few finely chopped toasted almonds is interesting.

SALSA ALLA PIZZAIOLA

1 tablespoon olive oil
6 good-sized tomatoes
salt and pepper

2 or 3 crushed cloves
garlic
1 tablespoon fresh ore-
gano, basil or parsley

Heat the oil and allow crushed garlic to cook gently in it,
but do not allow it to brown. Add peeled and cut up tomatoes,
pepper and salt and cook fairly fast until tomatoes are cooked
through but not reduced to a pulp. Add a good tablespoon of
oregano, basil or parsley, and before serving add another
clove of garlic cut very, very fine.

Tinned tomatoes may be used if fresh are not available,
but for this sauce the fresh are infinitely preferable.

An excellent sauce to serve with beefsteak.

SALSA VERDE
Green sauce

a good handful of
parsley
2 anchovies
1 small cooked potato
1 small onion cut fine

1 tablespoon capers
1 small gherkin
1 clove garlic, crushed
salt, pepper and oil
1 tablespoon wine vinegar

Pound together in a heavy mortar all the ingredients except
the oil and vinegar until they form a paste. Slowly add
sufficient oil to render this to the consistency of mayonnaise,
finally blend in a tablespoon of wine vinegar, and serve very
cold. A little fresh breadcrumbs may be substituted for the
boiled potato.

PESTO

Pesto is a sauce of Genoese origin that finds its ways into many dishes; it is excellent with spaghetti, for instance, and a tablespoon added to minestrone greatly enhances the flavour. Any left-over pesto may be placed in a small jar, covered with olive oil and kept for some days.

3 cloves garlic
sufficient fresh basil
   to produce 3 tablespoons
   when removed from
   stalks and torn into
   small pieces
about 2 tablespoons fresh
   olive oil
	1 cup grated Sardo
	   cheese, but since this
	   Sardinian cheese
	   made of ewes' milk
	   is not easy to procure,
	   Parmesan may be
	   substituted

Pound the garlic and basil to a paste in a mortar, add the cheese and continue pounding until a thick paste results, then slowly add oil until you have a mixture the consistency of mayonnaise.

A few almonds, pine nuts or even walnuts pounded into the paste make an interesting variation.

RAGU BOLOGNESE

SUFFICIENT FOR 6

No book on Italian cookery would be complete without a recipe for this, one of Italy's most famous sauces.

8 oz. lean beef or mixed beef, veal and pork
1½ oz. butter
3 oz. streaky bacon
onion, carrot, a stick of celery, a crushed clove garlic
¼ cup cream

2 or 3 cloves or pinch powdered cloves
1½ cups stock or water, or for preference 1 cup stock plus ½ cup white wine
1 teaspoon tomato paste
salt and pepper to taste

A few chopped mushrooms may be added if liked, and if you have three or four chicken livers available, these, chopped, are a great improvement.

If you use a mixture of beef, veal and/or pork, the beef should predominate. Pass all through a mincer twice.

Having minced the meat, place in a stewpan with the heated butter, add chopped bacon, onion, carrot and celery, all of which can, to save time, have been passed through the mincer. Add cloves, and allow to cook until the meat has browned and the vegetables are a golden colour. Add the stock and/or wine little by little, add tomato paste moistened with a little stock, stir well; add salt and pepper. Cover meat with the liquid, lower heat and allow the mixture to cook gently for another 15 minutes. In one of the traditional recipes milk is used instead of stock, which results in a richer-tasting sauce, but this is purely a matter of personal preference. At the end of the cooking time add the cream and mix well.

This is an excellent sauce for serving with spaghetti.

LIVER SAUCE FOR GNOCCHI

8 oz. liver (calves' liver will do, but chicken liver are preferable)
½ pint chicken stock
2 oz. butter
4 oz. button mushrooms
1 gill white wine
1 tablespoon flour
salt and pepper

Chop and flour liver, chop mushrooms small, and sauté both in butter in a heavy pan for 10 to 12 minutes, season with salt and pepper, stir in any balance of flour, and slowly add the wine; allow to cook 7 or 8 minutes longer before adding the stock. Simmer until thick.

APPLE SAUCE

4 cooking apples, medium size
1 teaspoon lemon juice
½ teaspoon grated lemon rind
salt

Peel apples, cut them into small pieces and place in a stew-pan with water to cover, and allow to cook until they can be mashed into a purée. Add grated lemon rind and a pinch of salt, remove from heat, and stir in lemon juice and mix well. Serve with roast pork.

BREAD SAUCE

1 medium sized onion	½ pint milk
stuck with 4 cloves	white bread
	½ oz. butter

Place the onion stuck with cloves and the milk in a saucepan and bring to the boil, allow to cook slowly for 5 minutes, then remove the onion and add enough white breadcrumbs to make a fairly thick sauce; mix well; remove from stove and stir in the butter and, if available, a tablespoon of cream.

Serve with roast chicken.

MAYONNAISE

Legend has it that a certain Duke of Mayenne, a great gourmet, was so busy discussing with the camp chef the preparation of a special sauce to grace a cold chicken that by the time the discussion had come to an end, his own cavalry had been overcome by those of the enemy, and the Battle of Arques was lost for his side. So much for history; the Duke deserves an honourable mention, for the sauce that caused the trouble was the forerunner of Mayonnaise, and took its name from the unfortunate gentleman who had a hand in its creation.

For a good mayonnaise you will need:

½ pint good olive oil	3 egg yolks
a pinch of salt	about 3 teaspoons lemon
	juice or wine vinegar

Place the egg yolks and a pinch of salt in a bowl and with a wooden spoon or a metal egg whisk beat them slowly, slowly until thick, and then start adding your olive oil, literally drop by drop. After 2 or 3 tablespoons have been added, the mayonnaise may be a trifle too thick, in which case beat in a little lemon juice or wine vinegar. Continue beating and adding oil slowly until the desired consistency is obtained.

SALSA REMOULADE

To a mayonnaise made as in the foregoing recipe add the following:

- 1 tablespoon made mustard — or to taste
- 2 tablespoons finely chopped capers
- 1 tablespoon finely chopped parsley
- 2 or 3 chopped gherkins

Excellent to serve with cold meat or with shellfish.

DRESSING FOR GREEN SALAD
SUFFICIENT FOR SALAD FOR 4

- ½ teaspoon salt
- 1 teaspoon French mustard
- 1 tablespoon wine vinegar
- 1 teaspoon castor sugar freshly ground black pepper
- 3 tablespoons olive oil

Mix together all ingredients except the oil, then slowly add the oil, and mix till well blended. An excellent mixer is of the type sold for mixing such drinks as Horlicks or Ovaltine. The mixing time is 2 or 3 minutes, and the dressing is all the better if it is made an hour in advance of the meal at which it is to be used. Once blended it can be embellished by the addition of a teaspoon or more of finely chopped parsley, mint or basil, and by ½ clove of garlic very finely chopped, if liked. Do not add to your salad until a moment or two before serving.

CHICKEN SAUCE

TO SERVE 4

½ pint cream
2 oz. Bel Paese cheese
4 oz. cream cheese

6 oz. cooked breast of
chicken cut in dice
4 oz. mushrooms
2 oz. butter

Place cream and cheese in a double boiler and cook slowly over hot water, stirring constantly until the mixture is smooth and creamy. Meanwhile, sauté the chopped mushrooms in the butter, add these and the chopped chicken to the sauce; mix well and serve hot over any kind of *pasta asciutta*. Grated Parmesan cheese sprinkled over the finished dish is an improvement.

PEA SAUCE

To serve with macaroni or with rice

1 onion chopped finely
1 rasher of streaky bacon
½ pint chicken stock
salt and pepper to taste

3 tablespoons olive oil
1 lb. peas (before shelling)
1 tablespoon parsley
chopped fine

Heat olive oil in heavy pan, and in it cook the onion until it is golden colour; cut bacon small and add, allowing it to cook for 3 or 4 minutes. Add stock, peas and seasoning, and cook slowly for 15 or 20 minutes.

HAM SAUCE WITH CREAM

TO SERVE 4

4 oz. lean ham or cooked
gammon cut small

2 oz. butter
½ pint cream

Melt the butter in a heavy pan, add the ham or gammon and allow to brown slightly before adding the cream. Lower heat, and cook together until the mixture begins to bubble. This sauce is delicious served over freshly cooked pasta of any variety.

MUSHROOM AND TOMATO SAUCE

SUFFICIENT FOR 6

1 lb. mushrooms
1 medium sized tin to-
matoes
3 tablespoons olive oil
1 clove garlic — crushed
cayenne pepper to taste

1 tablespoon chopped
basil, or if not avail-
able an equal quantity
of finely chopped
mint or parsley
pinch chopped thyme
pinch salt

Heat oil and in it allow the crushed garlic to brown; add mushrooms, sliced finely and simmer for 10 minutes; pass tomatoes through a sieve, and add to the sauce together with the remaining ingredients. Cover and allow to cook very slowly for an hour, stirring from time to time. Serve very hot as a sauce with any type of pasta.

MEAT SAUCE

FOR SERVING OVER SPAGHETTI

2 tablespoons tomato purée
1 clove garlic, crushed
¼ pint dry white wine
1 bay leaf
salt and pepper

2 tablespoons olive oil
1½ cups warm water
1 onion, chopped fine
8 oz. lean beef passed
   twice through mincer

Heat oil and in it brown onion and garlic and meat, add tomato paste and cook for a further 5 minutes before adding pepper, salt, bay leaf, water and wine. Cover and allow to cook slowly for 1 hour, stirring from time to time; remove bay leaf and cook a few minutes longer before serving with spaghetti.

MEAT SAUCE WITH MUSHROOMS

8 oz. lean beef passed
   twice through mincer
2 tablespoons olive oil
1 tablespoon tomato
   purée
pinch cayenne

4 oz. mushrooms, washed
   and sliced thinly
1 clove garlic, crushed
1 medium size tin tomatoes
salt and pepper

Heat oil in heavy pan, add mushrooms, garlic, cayenne, meat and simmer for 5 minutes; strain tomatoes and add, simmer gently for 45 minutes, blend tomato purée with a little water, add to first mixture, together with salt, cover and cook slowly a further 30 minutes, stirring from time to time. Keep hot till time to use.

CAPER SAUCE

TO BE SERVED HOT WITH ANY FISH

2 tablespoons capers
1 tablespoon flour
1 tablespoon chopped
 parsley
salt and pepper

2 oz. butter
2 tablespoons wine
 vinegar
¼ pint beef stock

Drain capers and chop finely; heat butter in heavy pan, add flour, stirring until it is smooth and has turned a golden brown; stir in capers, add vinegar slowly, and finally stir in parsley and seasoning, finishing up with the beef stock. Simmer for 15 minutes and serve hot.

SWEET SOUR SAUCE

FOR SERVING WITH VEGETABLES OR WITH FISH DISHES

4 oz. granulated sugar
1 tablespoon flour
2 tablespoons wine
 vinegar

¼ pint hot water
½ pint stock
salt and pepper

Brown sugar in heavy pan, sprinkle flour over and blend together; add hot water slowly, following with stock, vinegar and seasonings. Allow to cook 2 or 3 minutes and serve hot.

SWEET SOUR SAUCE WITH NUTS

TO SERVE WITH MEAT OR GAME

12 oz. chopped nuts, preferably almonds or pine nuts

2 squares unsweetened chocolate

2 tablespoons granulated sugar

3 tablespoons red currant jelly

2 tablespoons sultanas

the grated rind of a ½ lemon and ½ orange

½ pint stock

¼ pint wine vinegar

Allow sugar to caramelise slightly in heavy pan before stirring in grated chocolate and other ingredients. Simmer for 30 minutes, seasoning with pepper and salt to taste.

YET ANOTHER SWEET-SOUR SAUCE

TO SERVE WITH MEATS

2 tablespoons butter

pinch salt

2 tablespoons wine vinegar

2 tablespoons flour

fresh ground black pepper

½ pint stock or hot water in which vegetables have been cooked

2 tablespoons granulated sugar

Caramelise sugar and blend in flour, adding slowly the rest of the ingredients, and cook together slowly for 20 minutes before serving.

TUNNY SAUCE WITH BLACK OLIVES

TO SERVE 4

tomato sauce — (see any
of the various recipes
for this on pages 217—8)

4 oz. black olives
1 medium sized tin of
tunny fish
6 or 8 anchovies

Having prepared your tomato sauce, stone and chop the
olives, mash the tunny and anchovies, and add to the sauce
while it is still cooking; mix well, and serve hot over fresh
cooked pasta.

MARINARA SAUCE

TO SERVE 4

1 medium sized onion
4 tablespoons olive oil
½ pint white wine
1 pint shrimps

1 clove garlic, crushed
6 tomatoes, peeled
½ teaspoon brown sugar
salt and pepper to taste

Heat the oil in a heavy pan and in it cook the chopped onion
and crushed garlic until golden colour; add tomatoes, cut
small, together with sugar and pepper and salt. Lower heat
and allow to cook gently for 20 minutes. While this is cooking,
peel shrimps, and add them together with the wine to the
tomato mixture, cooking gently together for 15 minutes.
A little chopped fresh basil may be added 5 minutes before
the end of the cooking time, or failing this, chopped parsley.

Serve hot over pasta of any type.

A VENETIAN SAUCE FOR FISH

2½ oz. butter
4 oz. meat
  (preferably chicken)
¼ pint fish stock

1 tablespoon flour
salt and pepper
green colouring

Place half the butter in a small saucepan and allow to melt but not to brown; blend in the flour, and very slowly add meat and fish stock, stirring all the time until thick. Lower heat and add the remainder of the butter, a very little knob at a time, and when all used up and the sauce is thick, remove from the fire, stir in the green colouring and serve.

ANCHOVY SAUCE

10 to 12 anchovy fillets
  pounded to a paste
1 clove garlic, crushed
yolks of 4 hard-boiled
  eggs

2 tablespoons tarragon
  vinegar
2 tablespoons best olive oil
4 tablespoons parsley,
  chopped fine

Heat oil in a heavy pan, add pounded anchovies and crushed garlic, and cook slowly for 5 minutes; add parsley, vinegar and pounded egg yolks, stirring constantly until well blended. Remove from fire and serve very cold. A good sauce to serve with cold meats or fish.

Index of Recipes